THE COMPLETE IDIOT'S GUIDE® TO

Raising Goats

by Ellie Winslow

ALPHA

A member of Penguin Group (USA) Inc.

ALPHA BOOKS

Published by the Penguin Group

Penguin Group (USA) Inc., 375 Hudson Street, New York, New York 10014, USA

Penguin Group (Canada), 90 Eglinton Avenue East, Suite 700, Toronto, Ontario M4P 2Y3, Canada (a division of Pearson Penguin Canada Inc.)

Penguin Books Ltd., 80 Strand, London WC2R 0RL, England

Penguin Ireland, 25 St. Stephen's Green, Dublin 2, Ireland (a division of Penguin Books Ltd.)

Penguin Group (Australia), 250 Camberwell Road, Camberwell, Victoria 3124, Australia (a division of Pearson Australia Group Pty. Ltd.)

Penguin Books India Pvt. Ltd., 11 Community Centre, Panchsheel Park, New Delhi—110 017, India

Penguin Group (NZ), 67 Apollo Drive, Rosedale, North Shore, Auckland 1311, New Zealand (a division of Pearson New Zealand Ltd.)

Penguin Books (South Africa) (Pty.) Ltd., 24 Sturdee Avenue, Rosebank, Johannesburg 2196, South Africa

Penguin Books Ltd., Registered Offices: 80 Strand, London WC2R 0RL, England

Copyright © 2011 by Ellie Winslow

International Standard Book Number: 978-1-61564-018-8
Library of Congress Catalog Card Number: 2009941618

13 12 11   8 7 6 5 4 3 2 1

Interpretation of the printing code: The rightmost number of the first series of numbers is the year of the book's printing; the rightmost number of the second series of numbers is the number of the book's printing. For example, a printing code of 11-1 shows that the first printing occurred in 2011.

Printed in the United States of America

Note: This publication contains the opinions and ideas of its author. It is intended to provide helpful and informative material on the subject matter covered. It is sold with the understanding that the author and publisher are not engaged in rendering professional services in the book. If the reader requires personal assistance or advice, a competent professional should be consulted.

The author and publisher specifically disclaim any responsibility for any liability, loss, or risk, personal or otherwise, which is incurred as a consequence, directly or indirectly, of the use and application of any of the contents of this book.

Most Alpha books are available at special quantity discounts for bulk purchases for sales promotions, premiums, fund-raising, or educational use. Special books, or book excerpts, can also be created to fit specific needs.

For details, write: Special Markets, Alpha Books, 375 Hudson Street, New York, NY 10014.

Publisher: *Marie Butler-Knight*

Associate Publisher: *Mike Sanders*

Senior Managing Editor: *Billy Fields*

Acquisitions Editor: *Tom Stevens*

Senior Development Editor: *Christy Wagner*

Production Editor: *Kayla Dugger*

Copy Editor: *Jan Zoya*

Cover Designer: *Rebecca Batchelor*

Book Designers: *William Thomas, Rebecca Batchelor*

Indexer: *Angie Bess*

Layout: *Brian Massey*

Proofreader: *John Etchison*

Contents

Appendixes

Introduction

So goats have caught your attention—I don't blame you! They're the right size, reasonably priced, and productive creatures who have been serving humans for thousands of years. Small wonder you're thinking about raising goats yourself! When you're finished with this book, you'll have a pretty good idea about how to successfully raise goats and the enormous value they'll bring to your life.

Dairy and fiber goats arrived in this country with the first Europeans, but 1904 marks the official beginning of goats as an industry, and meat goats are relative newcomers since the 1980s. Thanks to the past 100+ years, the nature and needs of goats are well known. Your own journey with these amazing animals will be more fun and successful if you take advantage of the wealth of knowledge and experience of those who have gone before—both goat owners and scientists.

Choosing the right goats for you, your situation, and your expectations is the first step to a successful relationship. If you choose a goat who does not fit you, your goals, or your personality, neither you nor the goat is going to be happy. And although goats are generally hardy, they have their own particular needs you'll have to accommodate for the best experience. Having the insider information in the following pages will help you make the best decisions for human and goat alike, right from the start.

This book is for the goat lover, who is not an idiot at all, who knows little or nothing about goats—but is focused on shortening the learning curve. Welcome! You've come to the right place. Best wishes for a fun, fruitful, and fitting goat experience.

Extra Bits

Throughout the book, you'll see sidebars that contain additional information. Here's what to look for:

DEFINITION

New vocabulary comes with the goat territory. Look to these sidebars for goat-related terms and phrases you might not be familiar with.

GOAT HORN

Raising goats can be tricky at times. Check these sidebars for cautionary notes about possible trouble spots—the things that can maim or kill goats or cause serious problems for you.

HERD HINT

These sidebars offer tips and hints to save you time, money, or frustration and make raising goats nothing but smooth sailing.

KIDDING AROUND

Fun and interesting information about goats abounds. These sidebars share some fun facts you might enjoy and stories that illustrate "goatness."

Acknowledgments

No one writes a book alone. That's especially true with the one you hold in your hands. I'm deeply indebted to all the people who have volunteered to help because they truly love goats and want others to have a great goat experience.

My sincere thanks go out to all the people, too numerous to mention, who have contributed photographs for this book. Special thanks to Pat Showalter and Nathaniel and Colette Kemper for specific photos I requested. I appreciate the artists who contributed drawings: Peter Fetzer, Hank Kemper, and Veralyn Srch-Harelson.

Thanks to Mary Kellogg for help on both editing and factual accuracy, and to William Fetzer for technical support. Sue Weaver was invaluable in nontechnical support, and Ken Feaster-Eytchison provided help and friendship above and beyond.

Over the years, hundreds of people have freely shared information, techniques, theories, and practical goat knowledge. The goat community is full of remarkable people who truly have in mind the best interests of goats and the people who enjoy and love them.

Finally, special thanks are due to my mother, who early on in my life instilled a love of animals great and small and an appreciation for the joys of rural living!

Special Thanks to the Technical Reviewer

The Complete Idiot's Guide to Raising Goats was reviewed by an expert who double-checked the accuracy of what you'll learn here, to help us ensure that this book gives you everything you need to know about raising happy, healthy goats. Special thanks are extended to Kennon D. Feaster-Eytchison.

Ken Feaster-Eytchison resides in Idaho and has been raising and breeding goats for more than 30 years. He and his family currently maintain a small herd of Nigerian Dwarves and LaManchas. Ken serves as a director of the American Dairy Goat Association and actively volunteers his time to the American Nigerian Dwarf Dairy Association and as a 4-H leader in his community.

Trademarks

All terms mentioned in this book that are known to be or are suspected of being trademarks or service marks have been appropriately capitalized. Alpha Books and Penguin Group (USA) Inc. cannot attest to the accuracy of this information. Use of a term in this book should not be regarded as affecting the validity of any trademark or service mark.

So You Want to Raise Goats

In This Chapter

- An overview of goats throughout history
- Amazingly productive goats
- The differences among goat breeds
- A look at some favorite breeds

Making the decision to raise goats is a big one. What a journey you're about to embark upon! But as with any journey, this one is only as good as the knowledge and preparation that goes into it. That's where this book comes in. Consider it your goat travelogue. Besides wishing you a great experience on your goat journey, I also wish your goats a great experience. They deserve a home where their needs are met in safe and productive ways—a home that will appreciate their unique qualities.

Because you chose goats, I can guess a few things about you. You're concerned about the value and security of the lifestyle you live. You're probably concerned about the environment and the carbon footprint you leave. Maybe nutrition is important to you. Or maybe you're an independent thinker and love the creativity of your independence. Chances are very good crafts or arts feature in your life in an important way. Nature speaks to you, and you're probably surrounded with pets or other animals.

You've looked at all your options for more of the health and independence you want. You've correctly realized that goats are going to help you get it, do it well, and do it for a whole lot less than any other livestock can even come close to. Congratulations! You've made a wonderful decision.

Goats Around the World

Goats have been around for a long time, probably at least 10,000 years. Humans domesticated goats before sheep and cattle—and maybe even before dogs!—probably in the highlands of Western Iran. Our association with goats is long because it has served both goats and man well. They've provided survival for us, and we've protected them from predators and made their life a little easier.

Because goats were widely traded in ancient times, they spread rapidly into Europe, Asia, and Africa. Depending on the people and what they wanted or needed, they selectively bred their goats for traits that served them well:

- Dairy in Europe

- Angora in Turkey

- Cashmere in Asia

- Meat in Spain and South Africa

- Miniatures in West Africa

No matter what their specialties, goats provide multiple products and services. Goats supply milk, cheese, butter, meat, fiber, leather, fertilizer, and labor. In addition, they're hardy, intelligent, resourceful, sociable, entertaining, and inquisitive. These characteristics also make goats great companions.

KIDDING AROUND

There are about 700 million goats in the world. Twenty percent of the world's goat milk comes from Europe. France, for instance, has 3,500 goat dairy herds and 1.1 million goats, but they're only the fifth-highest commercial producer in the world. (Greece is highest.) Goats also provide food for millions. Far more people in the world eat goat meat and drink goat milk than eat beef and drink cow's milk.

Goats in Culture

You may not be immediately aware of all the places goat products and goat references show up in our culture, but they are ever-present if you stop and look.

The Latest in Goat Fashion

You might think only sheep provide fiber (a.k.a. wool), but goats do, too. Mohair, from the Angora goat, has been around since prebiblical times. It's known for its luster, sheen, flame resistance, and ability to retain its shape. Mohair is used in outer wear, furniture coverings, saddle cinches, and especially for doll hair and collectable teddy bears. It's often found in blends with wool and silk.

And then there's cashmere. Who among us hasn't at one time or another admired a cashmere sweater for its luxurious softness? First popularized by Lana Turner in a 1937 film, cashmere sweaters have long symbolized luxury and haute couture. Cashmere comes from the undercoat of cashmere goats and is a thriving industry in many parts of the world, especially the Far East.

Kidskin gloves are the finest leather gloves. Often used by debutantes at coming-out cotillions, kidskin gloves are elegant, soft, and a symbol of high society. Driving gloves, golf gloves, and many others boast of the softness and durability of kidskin leather. Even if you've never owned kidskin gloves, I'll bet you know exactly what it means to treat someone with kid gloves—delicately.

Goat-Related Stories and Sayings

The parable of the sheep and goats is found in the book of Matthew in the Bible's New Testament. In it, Jesus speaks of separating the righteous from the wicked and compares the first to sheep (innocent, tractable, and trouble-free) and the latter to goats (if there's trouble in the herd, it comes from the goats). Any goat lover will tell you the characterization is a little unfair.

Do you remember the classic "Three Billy Goats Gruff" children's story from your own childhood, or have you read it to your children or grandchildren? Chances are you're nodding your head "yes" right now. It's a typical story of good over evil that children around the world have likely heard some version of.

KIDDING AROUND

"Three Billy Goats Gruff" has, no doubt, contributed to the use of *billy goat* to refer to male goats instead of the correct term, *buck.* It's hard to argue with a folk tale of such extraordinary popularity, though! (*Nanny* is often applied incorrectly to female goats. They are *does,* just like deer.)

A *Judas goat* is trained to lead sheep or goats to slaughter while its own life is spared. This phrase also can refer to a brightly painted World War II bomber used to form a squadron of bombers from various bases. The term is generally used now to reference betrayal.

Old Testament leaders symbolically laid all the sins of the group upon a single goat, the *scapegoat*. The priest laid his hands upon the goat's head, transferring all the sins to the goat, and it was then driven out into the desert to permanently remove the sins from the people. We now generally refer to a scapegoat as someone who is wrongfully blamed or made to suffer for the faults or actions of others.

"Getting your goat" is a phrase that probably originated from the early days of horse racing, when each race horse was stabled with a companion goat to keep it calm. If a competitor stole your horse's goat (or "got your goat"), the horse was less likely to be able to race well. These days, "getting your goat" refers to anything that causes great frustration or consternation.

Goats in Song

"Bill Grogan's Goat" is an echo song, where the audience repeats each line after a leader sings it first, popular around Boy Scout campfires. Rollicking and fun, "Bill's Grogan's Goat" has a variety of lyrics depending on when and where you learned it. See www.djmorton.demon.co.uk/scouting/songs/goat.htm or www.scoutorama.com/song/song_display.cfm?song_id=449 for a couple versions.

If you've ever watched Rodgers and Hammerstein's *The Sound of Music*, you're probably familiar with the yodeling song "The Lonely Goatherd" Maria (a.k.a. Julie Andrews) and all the children sang in the movie. If you want to sing along, you can find the lyrics at www.songlyrics.com/sound-of-music/lonely-goatherd-lyrics.

Goat Dairy Products

Goat milk is the milk of choice for millions of people in nearly every country of the world. Some people drink it because they're allergic to cow's milk; some drink it because it's available; but most drink goat milk because it's economical to produce, delicious, and nutritious. (See Chapter 9 for more on goat milk.)

In addition to goat milk, there's delicious, rich goat milk cheese, or *chèvre*, the epitome of a luxury and gourmet ingredient in the finest recipes. The goat milk cheese industry has grown by leaps and bounds, and the cheese is a favorite of *smallholders*, or goat owners, because it's easy to create a palatable product from household milk.

DEFINITION

Chèvre, the French word for "goat," refers to cheese made from goat milk. A **smallholder** is a holding of agricultural land smaller than a small farm.

Miscellaneous Goat-y Bits

Goats have been used as a dowry all over the world for millennia. This was somewhat removed from American culture until August 2009, when a Kenyan gentleman offered 40 goats and 20 cows for the hand of Chelsea Clinton in marriage. Hillary Clinton, to whom the offer was extended, thanked the man for his "very kind offer" and said she'd convey it to Chelsea.

Finally, there's goat roping or tying. Believe it or not, this is a professional rodeo event where a cowboy on horseback rides up to a tethered goat and must catch it, throw it down, and tie three or four of its legs together to demonstrate the tie holds for 8 seconds. This event attracts youth because it's less difficult than calf-roping or calf-tying events. I don't recommend trying this at home.

Many Purposes, Many Breeds of Goats

Before you go out and buy any ol' goat, stop and think about why you want goats. Different breeds offer different "perks," if you will. If you primarily want goats for their milk, look at the dairy breeds. If you want meat, you should know there are meat breeds that have a far heftier build to provide meat. Fiber artists have a host of fiber breeds to choose from. If your primary goal is companionship, you might opt for the mini breeds. For brush control, any breed will serve you well.

The primary purpose you want determines the breed that will suit you best, but the other jobs you have in mind for your goats might make a difference between the goats of a certain type. It's important to remember that all goats can be multipurpose to a great degree. Most people want a variety of things from their goats, and the choosing is easier if you're clear on your priorities.

For example, all goats give milk, although some give a lot and some give a little. Some milk is better for drinking, and some is better for cheese, but all milk can be used for drinking and for cheese. All goats can provide meat, even the little ones, although it may not be a huge amount. Some of the dairy breeds can provide a little cashmere in the winter, and the fiber goats can still provide some milk or meat, just not as much as some other breeds. The neutered males of any of the full-size goats and perhaps even the smaller fiber breeds can pull a cart or learn to carry a pack to help with some of the labor at your place or on trips in the high country.

KIDDING AROUND

Although there may be as many as 210 breeds of goats worldwide, most have never been seen in the United States or Europe. So in this book, I only cover the more common breeds.

I know I sound like a broken record, but it's important that you first decide what your main purpose is for your goats and then look in that group. Ultimately, you'll choose your goats because you like them for a number of reasons, not all of them rational. But start with the details of what a breed has to offer before you get hooked by a cute goat that's not the best fit for your goals.

Now to help you make an informed decision about the type of goat best for you, let's look at some of the common breeds.

The Dairy Breeds

There's a reason goat milk is so popular. It's easier to digest than cow's milk, and the fat in goat milk contains more *medium-chain fatty acids* than the fat found in cow's milk. Goat milk also has smaller fat globules compared to cow's milk, making it easier to digest. However, not everyone likes the taste of all goat milk, and some people can taste a difference between breeds. I can taste a glass of goat milk and tell you what breed it came from. Whatever breed you decide on, taste the milk first.

DEFINITION

Medium-chain fatty acids are the good ones. They're more easily digested than longer-chain fatty acids (triglycerides) and do not require bile salts or modification before digestion.

Here are the dairy breeds:

Alpines are a medium to large breed of Swiss ancestry, noteworthy for giving large amounts of milk. They are a staple of commercial dairies. Their personalities are very independent and they may be harder to keep fenced than some breeds, and they like to fight with herdmates. As in all the breeds, when the volume of milk goes up, the percent of protein and butterfat goes down, so Alpine milk may be some of the most "diet" of all the breeds. That affects the taste, too. Some families of goats might have off-flavored milk, so always try it first. Alpines have upright ears and may be colored *cou blanc,* or white front quarters and black hindquarters with black or gray markings on the head; *cou clair,* with tan, saffron, or off-white front quarters, or shading to gray with black hindquarters; or *cou noir,* with black front quarters and white hindquarters. They have other color combinations, too.

Alpines are known for producing large amounts of milk, so put them on your short list if you're looking for lots of milk.
(Jeff and Pat Adels, West Virginia, Champion Munchin'Hill Annie)

LaManchas were developed in the United States from a variety of U.S. stock and some Spanish stock with no ears. They're medium to large in size and not at all flighty. They have good milk production, and their milk tends to be higher in both protein and butterfat than the Swiss breeds (Alpines, Oberhaslis, Saanens, and Toggenbergs). LaManchas can be any color or combination of colors, and they have no ears. Well, they *have* ears, but they're very tiny. The LaMancha ear is referred to as a gopher ear or elf ear, depending on the length. (Gopher are shorter.)

LaMancha goats are one of the best all-around goats, perhaps because they developed from many breeds.
(Jenny O'Connor)

Nubians were developed from Asian goats from both India and Britain. They're the most popular breed in the United States. They're the largest of the dairy breed. As a group, they have the lowest milk production, but their milk has some of the highest butterfat and protein content and is the best tasting. As with any of the breeds, these things differ widely among individuals. Nubians come in every color and pattern combination and are noted for their propensity for spots. Their distinctive feature is their long, drooping ears and Roman nose.

KIDDING AROUND

Many people either love or hate goats based on their ears. Those who like the LaMancha's earless look claim it's the clean head that appeals to them. Nubian aficionados often cite the breed's long ears as the thing that appeals to them.

Nubians have a reputation for being the noisiest of the dairy breeds, but it mostly tends to run in families, so you might luck out with a quiet family if that's important to you. Nubians are also friendly and gregarious. They're often considered dual purpose and have slightly better meat potential than other dairy goats. Nubians are more likely than the Swiss breeds to have three, four, or more babies.

Nubians, with their large and droopy ears, are so popular, competition is stiff in this breed.

Oberhasli is another breed developed in Switzerland. Quiet, docile, and intelligent, the Oberhasli gives a respectable amount of milk. They're of medium size, have upright ears, and are deep bay (deep reddish-brown) to deep red in color with an occasional black. Oberhaslis were originally called the "Swiss Alpine." Development of this breed has made huge leaps in the last decade or so.

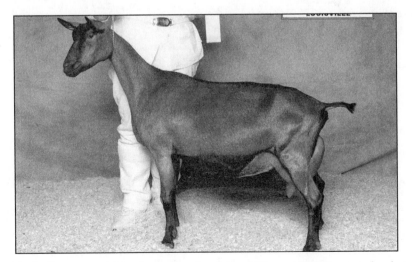

Oberhasli goats are often chosen first for their striking, reddish-brown color, but owners soon appreciate their other qualities.
(Sarah Love Davis)

Saanens are medium to large goats. They're placid and cooperative but perhaps less inquisitive than other breeds. They're known for giving the largest quantity of milk and are referred to as the Holsteins of the goat world. Needless to say, they're very popular in commercial dairies. Saanens are the breed with the most tolerance for getting a little wet. (Most goats like getting wet about as well as cats do!) If you like light-colored goats, this is a good breed to look at because they are all white or cream. The occasional colored goat goes into the Sable breed *registry*. Saanens have upright ears.

Saanen goats are known as the Holsteins of the goat world thanks to their high milk output.
(Kari Teampas, Kari's Kreations)

 DEFINITION

Registry refers to the organization that records purebred animals.

Sables are the Saanen goats who are colored instead of all white or cream. It's a fairly new registry to accommodate the purebred Saanens who carry the color gene. Their colors often resemble Alpines. Sables are large, productive, fairly placid, and have upright ears.

Toggenburgs are another favorite of commercial dairies because of their high milk production. As with the Alpines and Saanens, more production often means lower fat and protein. Also like Alpines, some families tend to have off-flavored milk, so try it before you buy it. Toggs are the smallest of the dairy breeds. They're also probably the most timid of the dairy breeds and tend not to run up to strangers. (They prefer sticking with both goats and people they're familiar with.) Toggs are fawn to chocolate in color with distinctive white facial stripes.

Toggenburg goats are a bit on the timid side, but if you like uniform patterns, you'll love these beauties.
(Mary and Bill Kellogg)

Miniatures and Crosses

In purebred registries, a special designation is given for goats who are crosses of two different purebred breeds. They are then in the "Experimental" *herd book.* Some outstanding crosses result from crossing one purebred with one of a different breed.

> **DEFINITION**
>
> The **herd book** is the record of all the registered animals of a particular breed and their ancestry.

Pygmies are small, stocky goats, bred primarily for pets, 4-H, and showing. They produce very rich, sweet milk in surprisingly high amounts for their small size. Production can be up to 5 pounds at peak, and butterfat ranges from 4.5 percent to more than 11 percent. That's creamy! Also, the stockiness of the breed means there's more meat for their size. Pygmies come in a variety of colors, and have upright ears and sometimes long, shaggy hair.

Pygmy goats are fun goats to own, and they're good milk producers.
(David and April Metheny)

KIDDING AROUND

Pygmies and Nigerian Dwarf goats both originated in West Africa. Although many disagree, it's believed they may have started as the same breed. At any rate, they were bred differently for different purposes in this country, and they've clearly diverged as separate breeds now. Both Pygmies and Nigerians are nonseasonal breeders and will breed outside of the traditional breeding season, sometimes twice a year. (See Chapter 6 for more on breeding.) Pygmies and Nigerians are the only purebred goats who can have blue eyes.

Nigerian Dwarf goats have only recently been accepted into the American Dairy Goat Association. They're officially recognized as a dairy breed, although many are still bred to be companions. Milk production varies considerably across the breed, but Nigerian milk is some of the tastiest, highest-butterfat, and highest-protein milk. Nigerians have upright ears, and any color or pattern is acceptable.

Nigerians are very hardy with few birthing problems and can have up to five or six kids at one time, although two, three, or four at a time are more common. Bottle-raised Nigerians are just as friendly as any of the big dairy breeds, but many are raised on their mother's milk and skittish.

Nigerian Dwarf goats are small, fun, and give milk that's like half-and-half.
(Ken Feaster-Eytchison)

Both Pygmies and Nigerians have been crossed with other breeds to create some interesting in-between-size goats who might be perfect for smallholders and homesteads.

Kinders are a cross between Pygmies and Nubians. They have been an established breed for more than 20 years. New Kinders are being made all the time with new crosses, but some lines go back to the original idea. Kinders are halfway between the parent breeds in size and appearance. They are dual purpose, used for both meat and milk. The milk is high butterfat and high protein, making it tasty and perfect for cheese-makers.

Cheese-makers, soap-makers, and people who like in-between-size goats favor Kinder goats.
(Pat Showalter)

The Nigerians have been crossed with all the full-size dairy goats now, establishing the group known as "minis." You can find Mini Nubians, Mini Alpines, Mini LaManchas, and all the others as well. For people who want a slightly smaller version of the big goats, these goats provide interesting options.

The Meat Breeds

There are two main meat breeds in the United States: Boers and Kikos. In addition, you can find indigenous goats of the Southeast, called Spanish goats, who have been crossed with both meat breeds.

Boers are big, meaty, white goats with red heads—although there are more color variations now as they've been bred more within the United States. Boers are shorter than the dairy breeds, and they are *far* wider. Boers haven't been bred or trained for long *lactations*, but their milk is rich in butterfat and protein—it needs to be to raise kids that gain about ½ pound of body weight a day! Boers originated in South Africa.

Boer goats are the Herefords of the goat world.
(Sue Weaver)

DEFINITION

Lactation is the period a goat gives milk, starting when her kids are born. Dairy goats tend to give milk for a 10-month period (usually 305 days) before they produce kids again and start over. Meat goats tend to produce milk until their kids are weaned, usually 3 or 4 months.

Kikos, the other meat breed, originated in New Zealand (or Australia) with indigenous goats bred to dairy stock and then selected for high meat yield, ability to survive with very little intervention, and breeding success rates of two kids weaned every year.

They are a large, often white, meaty breed with longer legs than the Boers and almost always with horns. Given their hardiness, they'd make great brush-clearing goats.

Kiko goats are the most independent and trouble-free of all goat breeds.
(Jim Stoltz, Midwest Meat Goat Network)

Breeds Best for Fiber

Angora goats originated in Turkey, and they produce mohair. Their fiber hangs in long, curly ringlets and is used for rugs, blankets, some outer clothing, furniture coverings, and decorative uses. Angoras are small and usually white, although breeders have now developed colored strains.

Angoras have been crossed with Pygmies to produce *Pygoras*, a breed with finer fiber than the Angoras that comes in several types. Pygoras have been further bred back to Angoras or to Pygmies, and a new group of fiber-producing goats has emerged, called PCA goats. (PCA goats are favorites among fiber workers. The *P* stands for "Pygora" or "Pygmy," the *C* stands for "color" and "cashmere," and the *A* stands for "angora.") If fiber is your thing, take a look at these small, fuzzy sweethearts.

Angora goats produce some remarkable fiber with many craft and commercial uses.
(Sue Muncey, Pleasant Hill Farm Angoras)

Pygora goats are treasured for their amazing fiber that wins many fiber competitions.
(Mary Donaty, Paradise Found Fiber Farm)

Cashmeres are feral goats selected for their undercoat, which is extremely fine and soft. The outer coat (called *guard hair*) is much reduced in cashmeres, but there are still some guard hairs that must be removed from the fiber so it doesn't cause itching when the final products touch skin. Unlike Angoras, which are sheared twice a year, Cashmeres are sheared just once, in January or February. Cashmeres probably originated in China, but today the name refers to any goat who produces cashmere. There is no registry.

My Favorite Goats

I've owned many types of goats in my lifetime but not every breed mentioned here. For the taste of milk, I'm very partial to Nubian and Nigerian Dwarf goats. Their milk is rich and always tasty. The higher butterfat moderates any off-flavors. I've heard from those who milk their meat goats and they say the same thing. (See Chapter 9 for much more about milk.)

For personality, I prefer Nubians and LaManchas. They're the most interesting, inquisitive, friendly, and least likely to jump fences or fight just for the heck of it.

For cuteness, it's hard to beat the miniatures. A newborn Nigerian Dwarf fits in a shoe box—sometimes even your hand—and still has all the bounce and capriciousness of any goat. And the kids are vigorous and aggressive about nursing from the time they hit the ground. If you choose to dam-raise the kids, they're easy. Nubian babies tend to be slow starters. For bottle-raising that's not a problem, but it takes them a while to get going on Mom. I'd hate to say they're dumb about it, but they are. This is probably a result of selecting cute over robust for 100 years of Nubian breeding.

I've never owned Kinders, but I love the statistics on these mid-size goats. They're the cross-breed of two high-butterfat and high-protein breeds, and their milk shows it. To check out some interesting milk records for Kinders, go to the breed registry website at www.kindergoats.com/milktest.htm. A goat who produces 2,190 pounds of milk in 305 days—as one did—averages more than 7 pounds of milk a day. (Roughly 8 pounds of milk equals 1 gallon.) All goats give more milk in the first part of their lactation and taper off over time, so this pint-size goat was probably giving well over a gallon of 5.7 percent butterfat milk (practically half-and-half!) in the beginning. That's some great cheese, butter, and drinking milk!

KIDDING AROUND

Why is milk measured in pounds rather than pints, gallons, liters, etc.? Basically, it's tradition carried over from the cow dairy world and because more butterfat makes milk weigh differently from less butterfat. Fat is lighter than water. Dairies get paid on a cwt rate (hundredweight) of milk.

The owner of that animal clearly knew what he or she was doing in selecting for good production, beginning with the first cross of a high-producing Nubian and high-producing Pygmy. I recently talked with an owner of Kinder goats who has an official *one-day test* record for milk production of 12 pounds of milk. That's about 1½ gallons of milk. That's a lot for a full-size goat, much less a half-size one!

DEFINITION

During **one-day tests,** over 24 hours, the milk of each goat is weighed, tested for butterfat and protein, and recorded for official production. The tests are sponsored by the U.S. Department of Agriculture, which keeps statistics and records on milk production.

Ultimately, most people buy the goats they like the looks of, and cute is always a big factor. But at least you now have some basic information about the breeds so you can make choices—beyond simply cute—that will suit you.

Goats have been human companions and survival help for many thousands of years, but they've woven themselves into our culture, language, products, stories, and songs. You are in good company when you choose to have goats in your life!

The Least You Need to Know

- Goats have a long history of domestication and companionship with humans.
- Goat references pervade our culture in products, language, song, and story.
- There are many breeds of goats, each specialized for particular needs (milk, meat, fiber, etc.), so you have lots to choose from.

Before You Bring Home Your Goats

In This Chapter

- Big things come in small packages
- Making space for your goats
- What shelter do goats need?
- *Do* fence them in!
- Checking some price tags
- Goat-proofing your land

After reading Chapter 1, you've determined that goats are, indeed, right for you, and you've narrowed down your choice of breed after carefully thinking about what purpose you want your goats to serve—milk, companionship, fiber, etc. Now let's turn our attention to what you—and your place—need before you bring home your goats.

By properly preparing yourself and your land, barns, fencing, and so on, you'll be better equipped to handle whatever comes your way on your goat adventure. There will always be surprises with goats—it's one of the things that make them so fascinating to own! Let's just ensure the surprises are all fun ones.

Goat Size and Adaptability

Goats pack a lot of productivity in a small package. For example, goats are small enough that even petite women and children can handle them with little concern for injuries or mishaps. And the difference between having a goat accidentally step on your foot and a cow step on your foot is *huge*. One might be uncomfortable; the other could break bones!

I recently conducted a survey among owners of some of the smaller goat breeds. They all positively noted the convenience and pleasure of an animal that's small enough to be easy in all management needs. Several brought up that they were still able to manage their goats, even when they (the people) have physical limitations. All mentioned that the smaller goats are more efficient in terms of space, needs, and production.

The adaptability of goats is legend. They can get used to large or small areas, a lot or a little intervention, different foods, and many different climates. These qualities make goats an ideal choice for small farms, homesteads, and rural holdings of many kinds.

How Much Space Do Goats Need?

Again, goats are amazingly adaptable. They can be comfortable raised in small pens or yards or roaming over hundreds of acres. Space simply isn't a limiting factor to having a good goat adventure. While their nature is to roam (more about goat nature in Chapter 4) and goats will enjoy acres and acres to wander about, they'll also manage very well in much smaller spaces. A friend of mine tells me she has 44 animals—goats, sheep, and other fiber animals—on 2 acres, and everyone's happy.

GOAT HORN

Although some cities have legislated goats as pets, not livestock, be sure to research the ordinances for your city before you buy any. Goats in the city present a few issues. Noise might be a problem. You'll need to keep the manure cleaned up to prevent flies and keep smells under control. And goats in your backyard might eat all your ornamental plants—some of which might be toxic. Do your research in all areas.

When you decide to keep animals in a small space, impeccable management is of the utmost importance to minimize the stresses and avert potential problems. The more crowded goats are in terms of space, the more important are things like hoof trimming, horns (to have or to not have), appropriate feed, appropriate mineral supplements, and your own observation. Noticing when something is amiss prevents little problems from becoming big problems.

What About Shelter?

Far more important than how much space you have for your goats is what shelter you have for them. What kind of shelter you need depends on where you live:

- In wet and cold climates, goats need protection from those elements.

- In deserts and hotter climates, they need some shade for relief from direct sun and heat.

- In areas with severe winters, a building, large or small that's at least partially enclosed, is necessary. You want to be sure the structure provides freedom from cold winds and wetness while still maintaining adequate ventilation.

- In very mild climates, they may need only a lean-to or overhead cover of some kind for shade and protection from rain.

Maybe you already have some structures that will work with a little adaptation.

Remember that in areas with severe winters, where weather may be "inside" weather for days or weeks on end, you'll need a bigger barn because the goats will spend more time in it. They won't go outside in rain, snow, or very stormy weather. They're probably not going to go outside if the snow is deep or the area is muddy. Also, the inside space—in most areas—will be where you feed hay because the food will stay dry and palatable out of the weather.

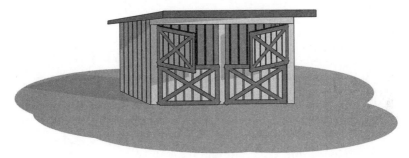

For areas with severe winters, a barn such as this will serve a few goats well.
(Hank Kemper)

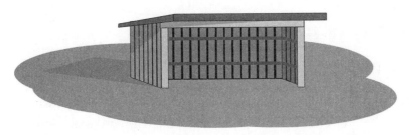

For areas with very mild winters, a more open shelter like this will work.
(Hank Kemper)

Milking Space

If you're going to milk your goats, you need a milking area separate from their living quarters so you can keep it pristine and ensure no contamination. It needs to protect you and the goat milk from weather and dirt. It's also good to have protection from insects, especially flies, which means screens and tight doors. Many goat owners create a milking room out of a section of the barn structure the goats live in.

Think ahead about how you'll bring a goat into this area to be milked and then put her back in with the herd. They know the milk room contains treats and are usually very eager to get in. Plan the layout so you don't have chaos at the doorway. Gates and doorways should always open *into* the goat pen. That cuts down on the crowding and possible turmoil a little.

HERD HINT

If you plan to milk your goats, you'll be carrying a container of milk from the location where you milk to your kitchen. Think about how far you want to carry a container of milk and any other equipment that needs to be cleaned. Keep in mind that 1 gallon of milk weighs about 8 pounds.

Kid-Rearing Space

If you plan to hand-raise any of the kids on bottles, you'll need a space for that, too. The kids need to be near where your milk and supplies are located.

Newborns on bottles will also do better if they're not in with the adult goats, especially for the first month or so. That shields them somewhat from parasites and aggressive behaviors by the other goats. When they're 4 to 8 weeks old and are eating solid food, they can be introduced into the adult pen if you wish.

Your kid-rearing pen can be in a part of your barn structure or free-standing. The young goats still need protection from rain, snow, wind, and blistering sun.

What About Fences?

The purpose of fencing for goats is twofold: it keeps your goats inside (and out of the garden, barn, back porch, and neighbor's alfalfa field or garden) and keeps other, unwanted things out of the goat area. The main offender is dogs, who can be deadly. There are other predators, of course, including the two-legged kind, and a fence tends to discourage them from plundering your goats.

Fencing to Avoid

You can use a number of types of fences with goats. But before we look at what you *should* use, let me emphasize what you *shouldn't* use.

First of all, do your goats have horns? A common behavior of curious goats is to stick their heads through fences (if they can). If a goat has horns, they can easily get stuck in many kinds of fences, so either get goats without horns or fences your horned goats cannot get stuck in. Friends of mine recently lost their valuable breeding buck when his horns became entangled in an electric fence and he couldn't get free.

Also avoid using barbed wire where your goats might try to climb through it, because they *will* try. Damaged udders can result from such climbing over and through barbed wire. A torn udder destroys a doe's ability to milk and may even cause death from a variety of complications. Barbed wire can sometimes be used in conjunction with other kinds of fence, but not by itself.

Good Fences Make Good ... Goat Pens

Taking these factors into account, let's look at what works for fencing in goats.

Woven wire is flexible wire in 4- to 6-inch squares (or smaller) and comes on a big roll. Woven wire is effective goat fence, but in areas near your barn or in high-traffic areas, goats can wear it out quickly by putting their front feet up on it—and they all will. High-traffic areas need reinforcing or additional strategies. Woven wire must be attached to real fence posts and stretched to be a useful fence, so it's far more labor-intensive than some other kinds of fences.

Electric fence is a cheaper alternative for fencing and can be effective at keeping goats corralled. It's often used in combination with other fencing such as electrified wire inside barbed or woven wire. Even straight electric wire can be effective, but it has some caveats:

- You must get high-quality equipment with plenty of joules (the measure of energy) and enough volts (what makes the energy flow). If your fencing is not adequate, your goats will risk the mild charge to escape. Please talk to an electric fence expert if you're thinking of using an electric fence.

- You have to keep weeds and grasses from growing up to the wire, or it shorts out.

- You have to teach the goats about it.

- It's not 100 percent effective at keeping out predators.

KIDDING AROUND

When there's something good to eat on the other side of an electric fence, I've seen adult goats push a youngster through the electric wire to break the circuit and create an opening for everyone else to get out.

My favorite goat fence is made of welded-wire *cattle panels* or *hog panels*. Cattle panels have uniform top-to-bottom openings, while hog panels have smaller openings at the bottom, making them slightly more predator-resistant and better at keeping in small kids. These fence panels are durable, galvanized, and welded-wire and are always 16 feet long. They come in various heights (for cattle or for hogs) and gauges. For the most part they're durable, but lightweight versions are cheaper and less rigid. And they're goat-proof, except perhaps for the miniatures and young goats.

Panel fences are easy to install with one or two *T posts* along the span. At the ends where the panels come together or make a corner, they are simply wired together, which is easy to do and easy to undo if you need to move the fence. The panels are heavy, but one person can move one around without too much trouble.

DEFINITION

A **T-post** is a metal fence post that's pounded into the ground like a big nail. You wire fence panels to the T-post for strength and to limit flexibility of the fence line.

You can also use the panels to create shelters or a covered area simply by bending them into an arch, anchoring it into the ground, and covering the frame with canvass or a plastic tarp. This is referred to as a hoop house.

I've also used *wooden pallets* for fences. Just stand them on end and wire them tightly together. Because the pallets are 4 feet high, goats can't escape … unless they're jumpers. And as an added bonus, foxes, coyotes, and dogs can't get through them like they might with cattle panels. If you zigzag the pallets, you don't even need posts, although I advise using some posts for more rigidity.

Wooden fences hold up to goats pretty well as long as they cannot squeeze through rails or panels. Remember that babies are much smaller and will therefore wiggle through smaller holes.

Whatever fencing you decide on, just be aware that goats love to get out and will if your fences aren't very, very goat-proofed. (See Chapter 4 for more on fencing.)

Look at the type of fence you choose from the perspective of how easily or not it can be breached by the kind of predators you have in your area. Few fences are really completely predator proof. If they're very hungry, many predators can go through, dig under, or jump over fences. Large carnivores can go through many types of fences. (See Chapter 7 for information on protecting your goats.)

The other thing to remember about fences is that they're not indestructible. Especially in areas the goats tend to congregate and put pressure on fences, the fences will break down. To be a good goat steward, be sure to check your fences periodically for holes, weakness, and other problem areas where your goats might escape or predators can gain easy access. Keep up on your fence-mending!

When it comes to fences, you ultimately need to balance function and cost—and do it before you bring home your goats or the result will be unpleasant for you, hazardous for your goats, and may cause conflict with your neighbors.

How Much Is All This Going to Cost?

There's no one-size-fits-all answer to this question. But let's go through some costs.

The Cost of Goats

An average registered goat of any breed costs between $150 and $600. The better the quality of the goat, the higher the price—usually, but not always. Unregistered goats can go for practically nothing, up to about $200. There are regional differences, too.

I strongly recommend getting a good understanding of what "quality" means— health, productivity, records, conformation, etc.—before purchasing any goat. (See Chapter 3 for a lot more about how to choose quality.)

The Cost of Goat Food

If you have to buy feed for your goats, and you probably *will* need to buy some even if you have many acres, find out what hay costs in your area and what the availability is. That will give you more information about costs. A full-size dairy goat needs about 1 ton of hay per year unless you have many acres of brushy or grassy land. And if it's raining they won't go out to eat it even if you do, so you'll need to feed them then. Check at feed stores, with other livestock owners, and with your county extension agent for possible sources and costs.

You also will need some grain for milking goats. The costs of grains go up and down annually, seasonally, and by location. A full-size dairy goat needs 1 or 2 pounds of grain at milking time twice a day, depending on her production. More isn't necessarily better, so calculate conservatively.

Other Goat Care Costs

Goats need a container for their drinking water. If you have many goats, you'll probably need a larger tank—or be forever filling water buckets all day! Some metal or plastic tanks made for cows or sheep are good for goats, too. But if you have only one or two goats, a plain plastic 5-gallon bucket is great. For smaller goats, find shorter plastic buckets so they can reach the water.

Inside small areas or pens, goats need some kind of manger for their hay. The simplest is just a tub to put hay in. If it's at ground level, the goats will probably find it fun to climb into it. That sure wastes hay! But a tub keeps it cleaner by keeping it off the ground.

KIDDING AROUND

Keeping goats from wasting hay is the holy grail of raising goats. They're notoriously good at it.

Here are some ideas for mangers that are fairly easy to build and at least help minimize hay waste. Visit other goat farms if you can, and look at what mangers are in use there.

A wooden keyhole manger works well for feeding goats because they must put their heads through the keyhole, or opening, first but then eat from the narrow part, which discourages wasting. These can be dangerous with aggressive breeds—if a goat is in the keyhole and they are hit by another goat, they could get their neck snapped before they could get out of the feeder.

(Peter Fetzer)

This manger is made from cattle panel sections. It's easy to make and keeps hay off the ground. (Do not use for goats with horns.)
(Peter Fetzer)

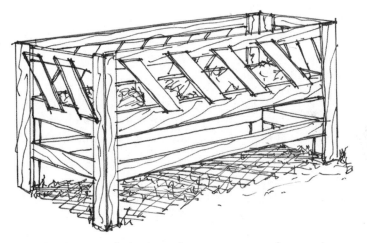

This slant-type feeder is another way to prevent hay-wasting.
(Peter Fetzer)

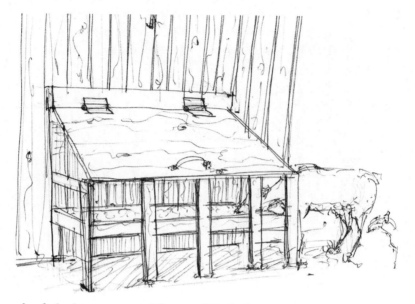

This wooden feeder keeps your goats' feet out of the feed and can be used for minerals or grain.
(Peter Fetzer)

If you don't want to build a feeder, some commercial manufacturers can provide what you need. Take a look at www.sydell.com/ProductCatalog/Product_Catalog.pdf, the catalog of Sydell's feeding solutions.

If you're buying a goat who is currently giving milk, you need to have a milking area and a milk stand. There are many types of milk stands, including some made of metal or PVC piping. Check online for ideas and plans for building a milk stand.

By now you probably know pretty well what you want goats to do for you, and depending on that priority, you may need several other pieces of equipment. Most likely, none of them is necessary before you bring home your goats and instead can be collected or bought as you go along. (See Chapter 5 for some other types of equipment you may need in the future.)

You can easily construct a milk stand from plywood and 2×4s.
(Peter Fetzer)

Goat-Proofing the Greenery—or Vice Versa

Goats are really good at eating weeds and shrubby plants (also called *browse*), but there are a few plants they shouldn't eat. Several plants are toxic for goats—some extremely so! Here are some widely acknowledged plants that can kill goats:

Azalea	Lily of the valley
Black cherry	Lupine
Bracken fern	Mountain laurel
China berries	Nightshade
Crotalaria	Oleander
Curly dock	Pokeweed
Delphinium	Red root pigweed
Dog fennel	Rhododendron
Eastern baccharis	Sumac
Honeysuckle	Virginia creeper
Larkspur	Yew

But this isn't all that cut and dry. Different sources report different toxic plants, and some lists vary depending on the region. I've seen goats eat bracken ferns with no bad effect, but that's only if they just take a nibble now and then. My goats loved black walnut leaves, although some lists say they're toxic. Rhododendrons and azaleas *are* deadly—period. Of the trees in the cherry family (possibly including pear and peach), the fresh leaves seem to be fine, but wilted leaves are toxic. If goats eat lupine, it may be fatal, but apparently the seed pods are the most toxic part of the plant. (See Chapter 4 for more information about what goats *should* eat.)

For more on what is and especially what isn't good for goats to eat, check out these websites:

fiascofarm.com/goats/poisonousplants.htm

www.ansci.cornell.edu/plants/goatlist.html

kinne.net/poi-list.htm

With all this information, you now know what you need to get your place ready to bring home your goats!

The Least You Need to Know

- Goats are small, manageable, and surprisingly adaptable.
- How much space can you devote to goats? Even if it's not much, they should be fine with the right care and management.
- Depending on the climate where you live, your goats will need some kind of shelter, from a lean-to in mild weather, to a fully enclosed bard for cold weather.
- Good fences not only make good neighbors but also a good goat experience for everyone.
- Be prepared to pay for the quality you want and the ongoing costs of goats.
- Toxic plants in the goat pen are bad news. Learn the plants that might hurt your goats and get them outta here!

Getting Your Goats

In This Chapter

- Baby or adult goats—what's best for you?
- One goat, two goats, three goats, four …
- Understanding inheritance and pedigrees
- Avoiding health issues and structural problems
- Goats R Us: shopping for and transporting your goats

Once you've made the decision to get goats, it's hard not to be so excited to get started you rush headlong into bringing home a goat or two before you do much of any planning or preparation. Whoa. Slow down. You first need to know some important information that will help ensure a better experience all around for you and your goats. Sad stories abound about people losing money and their goats getting sick or dying because they didn't have—or follow—some basic information.

"But," you say, "I have lots of experience with animals!" Well, that's good and will help you raise your goats, but goats aren't like most other animals. They may be as curious and friendly as dogs, nearly as smart as pigs, and eat food similar to cows or sheep, but they come with their own set of requirements and needs you *must* be aware of. Some of your experience with other animals translates well to goats, but not all does.

Should I Buy Babies or Adults?

Baby goats, called *kids*, are very cute as they bounce and cavort. In fact, that's pretty typical little-goat behavior, and it's highly entertaining to watch. The word *capriole* means "a vertical jump with a kick of the hind legs at the top of the jump"—the same jump little goats love to do. And that makes sense because *capriole* comes from the goat's scientific name, *Caprinae*, and the common grouping, *Caprines*.

DEFINITION

Kid is the proper designation for a young goat. ***Caprinae*** is the scientific name of the subfamily into which goats are classified.

No wonder the cuteness factor is one reason people cite for getting hooked on goats! But "cute" isn't the only reason you should consider one goat over another. There are pros and cons to both babies and adults.

Starting with Kids

Kids need milk until they're at least 12 weeks old, and it's best if they're not weaned from their mother's milk (or a bottle) until they're chewing their cud well. They can be raised on goat milk, cow's milk, or a commercial milk replacer. Real milk of either species is best to avoid digestive problems that have been reported with some milk replacers. Milk replacers made with milk rather than soy or grains are much less likely to cause digestive problems with kids. Do not scrimp here! At least half goat milk is preferable to a total milk replacer. If you have milk available to feed a young kid, a baby goat might work well as your first goat.

One downside of starting with a kid is that they won't be producing anything but cuteness for a long time. No matter what you want goats to provide for you, a baby goat is many months away from eating much brush, a year or more away from producing babies or milk, a year or more from being able to pack or pull a cart, and still several months away from butchering size. They can be very enjoyable companions, though, right from the start.

It's impossible to predict the level of a kid's future productiveness. The cutest kid might not produce much milk, fiber, or meat at maturity. Kids may not be as attractive as adults for possible show-ring activities. Or they might not get big enough for packing or driving.

If a kid really appeals to you, learn about its parents and siblings before you hand over any money. It's also helpful to learn more about how to spot good structure (more on that later in this chapter). But even if you do some homework, know there's often an inherent uncertainty with buying babies.

Starting with Adults

Beginning with adult goats brings less uncertainty, but there are still things to be cautious about. If you want a goat for milk and you buy a goat already in milk (already producing milk), the stress of a geographic move will decrease her production. Each animal is unique in the amount of decrease, but there will be some. If you're buying butcher stock, meat production won't be as much impacted by a move.

The advantage of starting with adults is that you'll have more immediate production of whatever you're looking for. If a doe has already kidded (had her babies) she'll be giving milk, even if the amount goes down some when you move her. If she's pregnant, you'll soon have new kids and milk production within a short time. By the time the kids arrive, the stress from the move will be over and her milk production will be up to normal. So if you're anxious to produce your own goat milk right away, then start with adult goats as your main goat purchase.

Starting with Both!

To combine the best of both options, perhaps buy a milking doe and her kids. Be aware, however, that nursing kids are reluctant to quit nursing and must be physically separated when it's time to wean them. There's a small risk that they may try to resume nursing when they're back in the same pen with their mother. In the following season, they even may try to steal milk from the newborns or from your milk bucket!

KIDDING AROUND

Goats have strong family bonds and long memories. A friend once asked me to board her goats while she was out of town. Some of her goats had come from my stock several years before, but not all of them. When she brought her goats to my barn, the ones not related to my goats knocked heads with mine and generally were disagreeable. The others, the ones originally from my stock, promptly found their mothers and lay down near each other. The family relationships still existed.

How Many Goats Should I Start With?

Only you can decide how many goats you should start with, based on what space you have and what you're prepared to handle. Ask yourself these questions:

- How much room do I have?

- How much milk (or meat or fiber) do I need?

- How much time do I have for caring for them?

- What are my long-term goals for my goat project?

Be honest with yourself when you're answering these questions. There's nothing wrong with starting with a few goats until you're sure this is something you want to continue with. You can always add more goats later if you really enjoy your goats. And because they reproduce pretty quickly, a small start can become a herd in no time so you might not need to buy more goats.

Goats can have a pregnancy every year—and some breeds up that ante and can have a litter of up to six babies! I talk more about breeding and pregnancies in Chapter 6, but for now, be aware that the twins, triplets, or quadruplets she produces each year can increase your goat numbers very quickly. Two starter females who each have triplets means that in one year or less you have eight goats!

The Nature of Inheritance and Pedigrees

Inheritance refers to something passed from parent to offspring—physical traits, personality characteristics, etc. But did you know various traits are passed on at various strengths? For instance, the *heritability* of the stature trait, or how tall a dairy goat is, is 52 percent. That's a very high number for heritability compared to some traits that are around 10 percent. So tallness in a goat depends a great deal on how tall her parents were.

 DEFINITION

Heritability is the degree to which a trait depends on genetics rather than environment and management.

How wide a goat's rump is has a heritability factor of 13 percent, which is a low heritability number. Low heritability means it takes a lot of time to make genetic progress. How wide the rump is depends heavily on other factors like environment and management rather than who her parents were.

It's important to investigate the family behind the goats you buy. Depending on what you want your goats to do, they should be able to do it well, without being sick, without costing you a lot of money, and for a long time. To one degree or another, many of the traits that help ensure that kind of success are inherited. If you can see the goat's sire (father) and dam (mother), sisters, or offspring, you'll have a better idea of how well the goat can meet your needs. A few hours spent investigating may pay big dividends in the long run. (Don't worry; I cover some of the traits that lead to good experiences later in this chapter.)

If few or none of the goat's relatives are available for inspection, the next best thing is pedigree information. Not everyone wants registered goats. If they are, however, they come with pedigree information that often provides some statistics available on the parents, grandparents, and beyond. Use this to help evaluate the likelihood the goat you buy will meet your needs.

Registered goats tend to cost more than unregistered goats. Record-keeping takes time and money, and you pay for both. Think about your future goat plans. If there's a possibility you'd ever like to show your goats or sell breeding stock, then starting with registered stock is mandatory. Not all registered goats are necessarily better than unregistered stock, but the statistics are in your favor.

Buy Healthy Goats!

Like any livestock, goats have a few potential health problems that can be chronic or acute. If you know what to look for and ask sellers about, you're less likely to bring these problems home with you.

What to Watch For

Of particular concern to the new goat owner are parasites, caseous lymphadenitis (CL), caprine arthritis encephalitis (CAE), hoof rot, Johne's, and pneumonia.

Parasites are ubiquitous. No one escapes parasites, but good management minimizes the problems they can cause. If you see goats that are thin, have rough hair, look listless with drooping heads, or are standing hunched up, suspect severe parasite problems. Other things might be going on, too, but parasites are nearly always part of health problems. You want goats who are alert, shiny, fat enough so their bones don't show through their skin, and walk smoothly without limping.

CL is a bacterial infection that causes pus-filled abscesses at sites of lymph nodes. The lumps are about the size of a lime or slightly smaller and often appear around the head, neck, and shoulders. CL is incurable, so if your goats get it, they have it for life.

It's also very contagious because the abscesses eventually rupture (if they're not lanced and cleaned) and spread the contagious pus onto ground, fences, and other animals. Pass on goats with lumps or scars around their head and neck that may have once been lumps. And avoid herds where you see lumps or scars. The CL bacteria can live for years outside the host, so contaminated ground and wood (fences, barn walls, etc.) can still be a concern even if left empty for a number of years. CL can cause death if the abscesses are in the internal organs. Although CL isn't usually life-threatening, it is something you don't want to mess with.

CAE is a virus unique to goats that can cause many symptoms, including arthritis, low milk production, encephalitis, and lung problems. CAE is passed from infected goats through *colostrum*, milk, and other bodily fluids. Goats can have the virus all their lives but not have any symptoms, or at moments of stress they can begin showing symptoms. Look for enlarged front knees and hard, low-producing udders. The diagnosis is reliably done through a blood test to see if the goat carries antibodies to the virus. Ask if a goat you are interested in has been tested for CAE, or what the status of the herd is. Many breeders practice CAE prevention, which is heat treatment of colostrum and pasteurization of all milk fed to kids because pasteurization kills the virus.

> **DEFINITION**
>
> **Colostrum** is the thick, yellowish first milk produced by mammals. It's full of antibodies that protect newborns.

Johne's is a chronic infection that localizes in the small intestine, causing a thickening of the intestinal wall, which prevents the normal absorption of nutrients. In goats, the symptoms do not appear until the last stages of the illness when severe diarrhea and wasting are evident. There is a blood test for Johne's.

Hoof rot is a bacterial infection of the feet and is most common when grounds are wet and the goats' feet are not regularly cared for. Never buy a goat who is limping.

Pneumonia is a bacterial infection of the lungs. All goats (and people, too) have pneumonia bacteria all the time, but it causes the disease when the goats are stressed, run down, or have other problems. Never buy a goat with a runny nose or one who's coughing. Pneumonia can show up after a goat is moved to a new home (remember, moving is a stressor) in which case it's sometimes called shipping fever.

I talk more about pneumonia, and all these other problems, in Chapter 8. These are just the ones you need to ensure you don't inadvertently bring home with your first goats.

Testing, Testing ...

The definitive test for degree of parasite infestation is a fecal test. It can be performed by any competent laboratory using a few fresh goat berries, or fresh stool.

You can conduct a quick visual test by looking at the color of the mucus membranes around the eye. They should be pink. Paleness or colorless membranes indicate a goat with high parasite load who is consequently anemic. That goat is going to be less productive and potentially ailing.

CL and CAE status are partially visual (lumps or swollen knees) but can be determined for sure with a blood test. I recommend you don't rely on visual signs to diagnose. CL lumps can be internal, and CAE can be nonsymptomatic.

Above all, don't be shy about asking questions. You're putting time and money into your goats, so you want the best of the breed. Decide how important these things are for you, if you are willing to invest in the tests, or choose breeders who are already testing.

The Importance of Good Structure

Assessing a goat's *structure soundness* can be difficult for someone who doesn't know what he or she is looking at. To make it easier, I want to talk about three systems that are important for healthy function and that are fairly easy to learn the basics of:

- Legs and feet (where the rubber hits the road)

- Back and rump (the structure that supports the weight of internal organs, babies, and milk storage)

- Udder (which undergoes extreme strain both structurally and physiologically when a goat is giving milk)

DEFINITION

Structure soundness is the components of a goat's skeleton that make her body work smoothly and healthily and give her longevity without aches and pains.

For our purposes here, we are concerned with soundness, not necessarily beauty. But as it turns out, a structurally sound goat is often more pleasing to the eye, too. A sound goat can be more productive and live longer, providing the activities, products, and enjoyment you paid for.

Structural soundness is the same among all breeds of goats. A meat goat and a dairy goat may have difference in the length of their legs or amount of muscling, but straight legs are structurally the same on both kinds of goats.

Leg and Feet Structure

Strong feet and straight legs are the basis of a productive goat because she can move around comfortably to get food. If her feet or legs hurt, she'll move less easily and forage less. Think of the legs on a table. They have to be plumb, neither sloping underneath nor sticking outward, or the whole table is off.

When seen from the front or the rear, a goat's legs should be parallel to each other. When seen from the side, they should be neither too far under the body nor too far in front or behind the body.

Viewed from the front, the front legs should be straight from the point of the shoulder down to the hoof with the knee centered and neither bowed in or out.

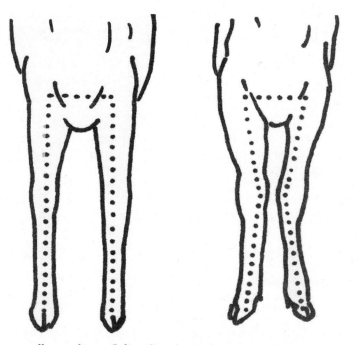

In a structurally sound goat (left), a line drawn from the shoulder through the knee should drop straight down and bisect the foot evenly. In an unsound goat (right), the line—and feet and legs—won't be straight.
(Veralyn Srch-Harelson)

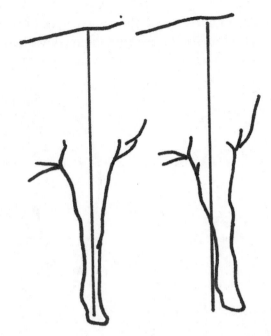

In a sound goat (left), the knees are straight and neither bowed in or out, and the leg is under the body adequately.
(Veralyn Srch-Harelson)

The back leg has a bend in it called the *hock*. Bent too much, it's called "sickle hocked," and bent too little it's called "posty." Neither extreme is good structure. A too-straight, posty rear leg tends to make the rear part of the goat higher than the front. It's unsound conformation.

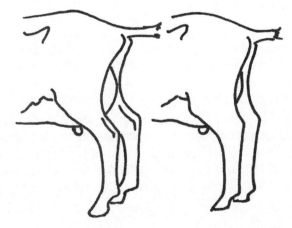

A correct hock angle (left) gives a goat a more comfortable gait.
(Veralyn Srch-Harelson)

Seen from the rear, the hind legs should be wide between the hocks. This makes enough room for a full udder so it doesn't get bumped with every step. Good width between the hocks makes the rear legs parallel to each other rather than angled in.

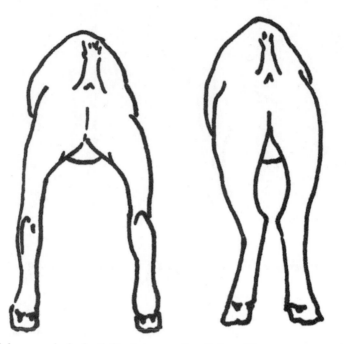

Good width between the hocks (left) gives room for all the milk a goat stores in her udder.
(Veralyn Srch-Harelson)

DEFINITION

The **hock** is the joint in a goat's back leg, similar to your elbow. The **pastern** is the short bone between the leg and the hoof. It should be at about a 20-degree angle. The **dewclaw** is the bump on the back side of the foot where the pastern connects.

A goat's toes should be of equal size and shape, with no crowding or extreme spreading. But perhaps the most important part of the feet and legs is called the *pastern*. The pastern is the shock-absorbing bone. It has a slight slope from the *dewclaw* forward to the hoof. When a goat walks or runs, the pastern moves up and down just a little to minimize the jolts. Short pasterns are strong pasterns. Long pasterns move too much and put strain on the ligaments and tendons that hold the foot together.

Over time, those stresses make the pastern relax into a sharper and sharper angle until the dewclaw is barely above the ground. Such a goat is said to be "down on her pasterns," and her feet probably hurt her most of the time.

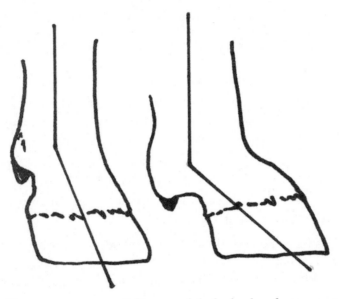

Short, strong pasterns (left) are good shock-absorbers for your goat.
(Veralyn Srch-Harelson)

Back and Rump Structure

Once the backbone projects beyond the bump of the *withers*, it should be without dips and curves. A straight backbone is sound and evenly supports the weight of her food, organs, babies when she's pregnant, and the pounds of milk she produces when she's *lactating*. If the back bone is "dippy" (sags) or "roached" (with an upward bump or curve), the goat probably is in some discomfort. An unsound back (or *topline*) crowds the heart and lungs. Poor structure also puts mechanical stresses on other parts of the goat's skeleton.

DEFINITION

Withers are the highest point of a goat's shoulders. **Lactating** means "producing milk." **Topline** is the name for the goat's back structure.

At the point where the back and hip meet, the rump starts. Long, wide, flat rumps with a slight rearward slope are ideal. A rump that's too steep decreases the birth canal space and can cause birthing problems. When viewed from behind, rump structure that slopes downward and sideways from the backbone makes a rump that's narrow side to side. Length, flatness, and width all mean lots of internal room for the kids to be birthed easily.

Udder Structure

The udder produces milk and stores it. Because it's on the underside of the goat, it's vulnerable right from the start. The ideal shape and structure of an udder is about keeping it safe from harm.

Poor udder structure might result in it hitting bushes or obstacles the goat walks over or around or even getting kicked by the goat's feet. A poor udder is more susceptible to infection from injuries and bacteria. It's also less likely to produce milk over a long lifetime, either for you or for her kids.

A good udder is tucked up tightly to the goat's body, not hanging low. Look at a goat from the side. The bottom of the udder (called the udder floor) should be high—preferably at the hocks or above. The farther down it hangs, the more likely it's going to get in the way and get injured.

Ligaments and connective tissue hold the udder to the goat's body, and the stronger these are (determined partly by genetics and partly by nutrition), the better. Strong ligaments mean little sway front to back or side to side. That's good.

The most important of these is called the *medial suspensory ligament*. It should connect forward on her belly in front of the udder, creating an extended front *attachment*, and high behind it, creating high rear attachment and separating the two halves. Too strong, and you have too much separation in the halves; too weak, and the udder floor has a rounded center, more like the curve on a basketball. Connective tissue on the sides of the udder hold it side to side. Poor side attachment appears as space between her hind legs and the udder when viewed from the back. It's all about support.

DEFINITION

The **medial suspensory ligament** is the connective tissue that holds the goat's udder to her body. It connects in the front of her udder and in the back through the center of her udder. An **attachment** is a ligament or other structure that attaches the udder to the goat's underside.

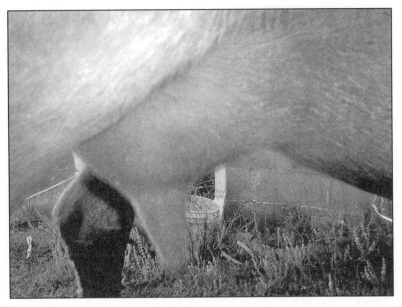

This fore udder extends nicely, so the udder will stay tucked up to the goat's body.
(Nathaniel Kemper)

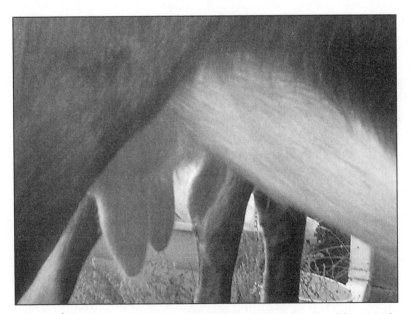

This fore attachment is very short, so the udder will hang lower and lower with age and production.
(Nathaniel Kemper)

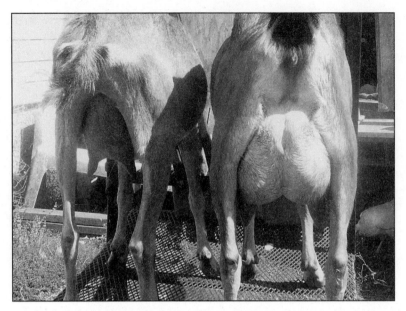

The udder on the left has very little side attachment compared to the one on the right. It will sway and bump her legs as she walks even though it's not as productive as the one on the right.
(Nathaniel Kemper)

On the udder, there's much variation in the size and placement of *teats*. If they're too far apart or too close together, it's hard to aim for the bucket when you're milking. Either might be fine for her kids. Teats need to be long enough but not too long, both for milking ease and also for just the overall esthetics of the goat. Judges in show rings have a specific look they go for—medium spacing and teats that point straight down because that makes for easier milking. If you're going to buy a goat who is milking, try milking her before you buy—with the owner's permission, of course.

DEFINITION

Teats are the "handles" at the bottom of the udder through which milk passes. The **orifice** is the hole at the end of the teat that works as a valve to keep milk inside the udder and opens under pressure to release milk. **Mastitis** is the name for any infection in the udder.

Another thing that can make milking hard or easy is the size of the opening in the end of the teat, called the *orifice*. If it's very small, she'll require more hand pressure to get the milk out. If the opening is very large, she may be prone to leaking when she's full of milk, but she'll be very easy to milk. Leaking milk is a medium that bacteria love to grow in, making infection or *mastitis* a concern. Mastitis is virtually impossible to cure once it's established. (See more about mastitis in Chapter 8.)

If you're buying a milking goat, get your hands (be sure they're clean!) on her udder. The udder should not contain any lumps or hard tissue. If it does, she probably has mastitis now or has had it in the past. Active mastitis means there's infectious material (pus) in her milk, and a diagnosis can easily be determined with a test called the California mastitis test (CMT). A purple reagent is swirled in a shallow cup with a small amount of fresh milk. If it thickens up, it indicates active infection. You can even make your own reagent using some dish washing liquid such as Palmolive.

Do not buy a goat with mastitis, ever! Or one who has had mastitis!

Goats with good structure are healthier and happier, and you will have a longer productive life from them. Try to look at many goats and specifically notice their feet and legs, back and rump, and udder so you can choose the best goats for your purposes.

Where to Buy Goats—and Where Not to Buy Them

You don't want to go just anywhere and buy any goat. At some places, buying goats is loaded with hazard. The worst is the sale yard or auction house. The auction house is where goats are sold for meat. Some of those, of course, are meat goats and may be perfectly healthy. Many are not. Sick goats and goats with structural problems, behavioral problems, production problems, reproductive problems, and others may end up in the sale ring. Statistics are against you getting a good goat there. Yes, they're cheap, but more often than not, they come with big issues.

GOAT HORN

Remember, when you purchase from an auction yard, your new goat has been exposed to every disease that has ever passed through there! In some instances, you can track many diseases by just walking through the sale yard.

Another place to avoid is the farm where the goats appear to be pretty much on their own and look scruffy, dirty, or skinny. Beware of people who refer to their goats as "billies" and "nannies" (remember, the correct terms are "bucks" and "does"). That tells you they don't know as much about goats as you need from a breeder.

In the ideal situation, the people you buy your goats from are at the very least going to be a resource for all things goat, and at most, perhaps they'll be your goat mentors. How do you find such people? Just keep reading!

Go to your local county fair and find the goat display. Look at the goats. Look at the people owning and showing goats. Ask questions. The county fair is a good place to see many breeds in one place so you can see what appeals to you. You can also get a feel for healthy goats because sick goats are supposed to be excluded from that venue. Just as a precaution, this isn't *always* the case. Some breeders have little regard for the health of their animals. It's important to look closely at the goats. Do they have slick or dull goats? Do their noses look snotty or clear? Do they look alert or droopy?

You may be able to connect with suitable breeders, goat organizations or clubs, 4-H leaders, Future Farmers of America (FFA) teachers, and county extension agents in your area. These groups offer a world of knowledge and experience.

No matter where you live, an annual sanctioned goat show or two is probably held somewhere near you in addition to the county fair shows. Contact arena owners to see if any goat shows are scheduled in their facility.

Watching a goat show can be a huge learning experience. Goat shows of dairy breeds, fiber breeds, and some of the meat breeds include something unique for the novice. When the judge places a class of animals, first to last, he or she then gives his reasons for the placement. You will hear comments such as, "One places over two for her strength of mammary system and correctness of feet and legs." As the onlooker, you can then compare the udder and feet and legs of the first-place goat to the second-place goat. It gives you a quick lesson in what good structure looks like with something to compare it to.

Or you may hear something like this: "Three places over four for her more correct topline and more nearly correct placement of teats." This comparison is about the straightness of the back and what good teat placement looks like.

As you can tell, a goat show is a good place to spend a day or two before you try to assess goat structure on your own. As at the county fair, talk to breeders, and look at goats in pens. See which goats take ribbons.

Here are some questions to ask any breeder:

- How long have you been raising goats?
- What conditions and diseases do you routinely test for?
- What do your goats eat?
- What vaccinations do you give?

If the breeders' answers are satisfactory, these breeders could be an excellent resource from which to buy goats. Even if they have no goats for sale (a rare occurrence if they're at a show), they may be willing to help you further. Of course, if you get unsatisfactory answers, definitely keep looking!

Finally, if you have a pretty good idea of the kind of goat you want, you can contact registry organizations to find breeders of that type of goat in your area. (See Appendix B for a list of registry organizations.) Visit several breeders. Ask the same questions you asked at goat shows. Look at goat relatives to see how traits are passed in families. Compare prices, too.

The more goats you look at, and the more questions you ask, the better your chances for getting goats that will meet your needs.

How Do I Get My Goats Home?

One of the nice things about goats compared with some other kinds of livestock is their size and adaptability. Many a family vehicle has carried a backseat of goats and children—to the amazement of other travelers.

When you're buying one or two goats, especially young ones or miniatures, it's fairly simple to transport them in a large car, van, or station wagon. The shorter the ride, the better, of course, and you should be prepared for accidents.

But what if you want to bring home a group of goats? Typically, they are transported in trailers, covered pickup beds, and other vehicles used for transporting livestock.

If the weather is warm or hot, goats are sometimes transported in pickup beds with wire cage sides. The cage is often made of tall fencing panels. Some have a roof; some just have tall sides. Be aware that wind speeds in a transporter open to the air will be uncomfortable and more stressful to the goats than an enclosed transporter. In very cold winter or wet conditions, this is not a good transportation method and you could have sick goats.

GOAT HORN

When considering how to get your new goats home, this is a good time to stress the benefits of buying tame goats. Regardless of what the transportation looks like, your experience will be safer and more successful if the goats are tame and easily handled. A wild goat who escapes during transportation may never be retrieved.

Getting goats into a trailer is usually very simple because they tend to be low to the ground. And if your goats are wearing collars, the handling will be easier, too. A goat can be led in, sometimes with a push from behind as she's being pulled from in front.

If you're trying to get a goat into a pickup bed, it will usually take more effort. Small goats can be lifted in. When you're working with full-size adults, a few will be willing to jump up into a pickup bed on their own, particularly if someone is enticing them with a little treat such as grain. If not, have one person lift the front feet up onto the bed while another person pushes from behind. When the goat's center of gravity shifts forward enough, lift the rear end into the pickup. Be prepared to close the door quickly for those goats who try to jump back down!

When you get the goats to your own place, getting goats out of your transportation is much easier. Most will be happy to jump out. Very short-legged adults (like Nigerian Dwarfs and Pygmies) may not be willing to jump out, and very pregnant goats or those with a full udder should not be forced to jump without your help. Keep a hand on the collar and then lead them into their new enclosure. If they have food and water available, they will find it on their own and settle in comfortably. If they are joining other already-established goats, expect some head-butting to establish hierarchy. Watch to see that no one gets excluded from the food.

Transportation is stressful on goats, and long trips are more stressful than short ones. There is a type of pneumonia commonly called shipping fever that sometimes results from the stress of moving goats. Watch for runny noses or coughs that develop after transport. Treat with antibiotics under the supervision of your veterinarian.

The Least You Need to Know

- Decide before you buy how many goats are right for you and whether you want babies or adults. And remember, goat herds can grow quickly, so don't buy too many for your needs or you could be overrun!
- You can't milk registration papers, but they may have a lot of value for your long-term goals.
- Learn what to look for, health-problem-wise, so you don't bring home anything with your new goats you don't want.
- By learning to spot a sound goat, you can purchase healthier, happier, more productive goats.
- There are good places to look for goats to buy but there are some to be wary of, too. Always keep your eyes open, and don't be afraid to ask questions.
- Transporting your goats is pretty easy, if you keep in mind a few considerations.

The Nature and Needs of Goats

In This Chapter

- Understanding goat thought and behavior
- What's on the menu?
- A look at goat personalities
- The pros and cons of tethering

If you want a great experience with goats, you need to learn as much about them as you can. Goats have personalities that will amaze and entertain you, but the same quirks that make you laugh could make you aggravated, or worse, if those quirks aren't accommodated. Not knowing the nature and needs of goats is a recipe for disaster.

Inadequate nutrition or poorly designed management sooner or later means your goats will have poor health, productivity, or behavior. You could have sick goats, dead goats, or goats in places they don't belong if you don't stay on top of your game. The learning curve is steep, but your effort will pay off in the end!

Goat behavior is unique among livestock. It's what makes them far more interesting than most other barnyard animals. Okay, okay, not everyone will agree with that last statement, I know. But read on about the nature and needs of goats and see what *you* think. I bet you'll appreciate their uniqueness and the way they think and act as much as I do.

Getting Inside a Goat's Mind

There are six characteristics of goats that can be pretty perplexing if you're not aware of and prepared for them. They're also the characteristics that make them fascinating to watch and observe. Once you understand how a goat thinks about her world, you'll both be happier.

Social Structure

The first thing you should know about goats is that they're herd animals. They have a social structure that always includes at least one other goat. If you buy one goat and put her in a pen or pasture all by herself, she may just stand at the fence all day and scream for company. Neither of you will be happy with this setup.

Goats need to live in groups of at least two, be it a mother and her baby or babies, a group of siblings, or a mixture of two or more adults. Always raise goats in a goat-social environment where they have other goats to interact with. It's kinder and much more pleasant for both you and your goats.

Pecking Order

Goats have a pecking order. One goat will always be "top goat" in a group. It can be pretty dramatic to see that hierarchy worked out at your place. If you bring two or more goats together who have not already figured it out, they'll certainly do it when introduced. They may rise up on their hind legs, butt heads, nip at each other, or push and shove. Such displays may go on for hours or days, depending, in part, on the breeds involved. This is normal goat behavior, so don't get upset. They're deciding their hierarchy. The boss goat will usually be the biggest or oldest, but not always. All goats, regardless of gender, will determine the boss goat this way.

KIDDING AROUND

Alpine goats seem to be the most prone to fighting with each other. Saanens and Nubians are the least apt to do so.

On rare occasions, goats can do some damage to each other, especially if horns are involved. (I talk more about horns in Chapter 5.) If this happens, the goats need to be separated by at least a fence or gate so they can adapt to each other more slowly—and out of each other's reach. They usually settle down in a few days.

Climbing

It's the nature of all goats—instinctively there from the time they're born—to climb. Goats love to get on top of anything in their area taller than ground level. People who have not understood this characteristic and happened to leave a new car where goats can get to it have horror stories to tell of the scratches and hoof-shape dents the goats left for them.

Goats like to play king-of-the-mountain with anything they climb on. They will always attempt to get to the highest point and keep any other goats from reaching the pinnacle. Because climbing is such an integral part of the goat personality, many people with goats create climbable toys (like a jungle gym) for their enjoyment.

In addition to climbing, you'll often see your goats putting their front feet up on things—walls, feeders, fences, and maybe even you! Of course, there are repercussions to this. Feet up on a feeder means the food can get contaminated with dirt and fecal matter. Feet on fences is very hard on the fence structure and integrity. Feet on you or other humans is cute when the goat is a kid. You only have to deal with small, dirty hoof prints on your clothes. But when a goat gets bigger, it's not so cute and some people, including children, could be at risk for injury if the goat is heavier. Start early teaching your goats not to jump up on people.

Goats of all ages love to climb on just about anything.
(Nathaniel Kemper)

Goats love a jungle gym.

Some people go all out when building climbing toys for their goats.
(Shar Miller)

HERD HINT

You can teach young goats not to jump up on you. First, you can simply move out of a jumping goat's way to discourage the behavior. If jumping persists, you can take a spray bottle of water into the goat pen with you and spray the jumper's face if she misbehaves. Goats hate to get wet, and they learn quickly with this technique.

Normal goat behavior includes butting each other, but you're not a goat, so never let your goat butt you or other people. Sure, it might be cute when a small kid play-butts you and you let her. But retrain yourself out of this notion if you have to. You don't want a goat who's annoying, not to mention potentially dangerous!

Curiosity and Fences

Goats are very smart as smarts go in the animal world, but their curiosity stands head and shoulders above other livestock. This can be a mixed blessing, especially if you're not prepared for it.

On the upside, animals who explore and are curious about the world are endlessly entertaining. They'll make you smile and sometimes laugh out loud with their antics.

On the other hand, that same curiosity can make them hard to keep where they belong. If your fence has a weak spot or a gap, I guarantee the goats will discover it. If you want them to stay away from something (like the garden), that's exactly where they'll show up. You know all those delicious vegetables and berries you love from your garden? Your goats will love them, too, along with your roses, fruit trees, and ornamentals!

To reap all the benefits of goat curiosity—and none of the frustration and problems—you *must* check your fences for weaknesses your goats can take advantage of or holes they might try to squeeze through. If you don't want goats in the garden, be sure it, too, has a good goat-proof fence. (See Chapter 2 for more about good goat-proof fences.)

In the areas near the barn, gates, and interaction with feed and people, your fences need to be especially strong. All that "feet-on-the-fence behavior" will wear out fences fast if they're not extremely durable.

Goats Hate to Get Wet

The degree to which goats hate to get wet varies a little by breed, but not much. Most goats out in the woods or in a pasture head for shelter at a dead run when rain or snow begins. Saanens have a little more tolerance for wetness, but not much. Goats do not like their feet wet, either.

KIDDING AROUND

On my farm in western Oregon, a small stream bisected the property. The far side was covered with lush goat food, but it was nearly impossible to get the goats to cross that 4-inch-deep stream. A couple of the younger goats finally learned to cross on their own, but they always did so reluctantly. Most of the goats had to be dragged or carried across and would never cross on their own even for the desirable reward of yummy blackberries and other brushy goat food.

Like any other goat characteristics, their dislike of getting or being wet factors into other things. Barns and shelters should be on high ground. Pathways into milking areas or places you want goats to go need to be on high ground. Not only is a wet goat unhappy, but it's also susceptible to upper-respiratory infections. Continually wet feet create the conditions for foot rot.

Following and Herding

Do you remember the 1937 movie *Heidi* starring Shirley Temple? In it, a girl takes her grandfather's herd of goats up the mountain to feed each day. She walks along, and they follow behind. That's a great demonstration of typical goat behavior. They love to follow "their" people or the boss goat. But nothing happens if you get behind the goats and try to push them in the direction you want them to go. They will simply turn aside until they get around behind you and wait for you to lead on.

Goats will also follow other animals. They are sometimes kept with cattle because the cattle eat grass and leave the bushes and weeds, which the goats clean up while they follow along behind the cows. If goats live with a livestock guardian dog (LGD; more on these in Chapter 7), they'll follow her.

Don't expect to drive or herd them anywhere. It just won't work.

What Do Goats Eat?

What goats eat ultimately determines their health and productivity. Just as humans are what they eat, so are goats. A little knowledge about what's appropriate and taking the effort to provide goat-suitable feed pays off in productivity and longevity.

Before we go much further here, let's dispel some myths surrounding what goats eat. If you believe everything you've ever read, heard, or seen about goats, you may be in for some surprises when you find out the truth. For example, you've probably seen pictures of goats eating tin cans. They don't! Nor do they eat just *anything*. They may have that reputation among certain cartoonists, but if you ask anyone who has been around goats for very long, they'll tell you what picky eaters goats can be. Of course, a hungry goat is considerably less picky.

KIDDING AROUND

Goats sometimes find paper pretty palatable! I've seen a goat eat part of a brown paper grocery bag or munch on informational handouts that have drifted near their pens at the fair. Those who think they've seen a goat eat a tin can were probably watching it eat the *label* off the can! It makes sense: paper is made from trees, and goats love small trees.

Forage

Goats are browsers like deer, alpacas, and elk, not grazers like sheep, horses, and cows. So although all these animals (except alpacas and horses) are *ruminants*—animals who have four stomachs and chew their cud—they don't care all that much for grass, although goats will eat grass when there's nothing more palatable.

Instead, browsers like brush, bushes, small trees, some weeds, and the bark of many trees. They're especially fond of blackberries, yucca, thistles, and rose bushes (both wild and domestic). This browsing nature of goats makes them great land-clearing machines, especially where lots of weedy and shrubby plants grow.

They'll also control many noxious weeds, like kudzu or leafy spurge, that might grow in your area. Some goats eat poison oak and poison ivy, but others don't like it.

GOAT HORN

If goats browse in areas where poison oak or poison ivy grow, they'll have the plant oils on their hair from brushing against these plants. Be careful about picking up these poisons secondhand while touching the goats. The oils will eventually wear off their coats, but in the meantime, protect yourself by wearing long sleeves designated only for handling the goats.

Browsers do a lot of traveling. They take a bite here and wander over to a bite there, covering a lot of ground. Browsing is generally several inches to several feet above ground, too. Remember that fact when you're considering how to provide other types of feed. Up off the ground is more in tune with a goat's nature. Cleanliness also comes into play. (I talk about this again in Chapter 7's discussion of parasites.)

A browser's diet is varied. Some times of the year, a plant will be particularly appetizing to goats, and at other times, they'll pass it by. A goat with an adequate browsing smorgasbord will probably be at top-notch health and productiveness, as nature provides the nutrients she needs within that variety.

With many acres of land, and in the perfect geographic location, browsing is ideal, but most goat owners must accommodate other considerations, too. Unfortunately, browsing is not possible in all climates in all spaces, in all seasons, nor for all people's needs. Even if you have great browse on your property, milk-producing goats will need supplemental hay in the evenings. They have huge protein and mineral demands 24 hours a day, and they should eat at night to help meet those demands.

Other ways of feeding goats can be practical in different situations. If you've ever driven by a pasture with a herd of grazing goats, for example, you've seen how many large meat goat operations manage part of their diet.

Hay

In winter months in most areas, there's little or no growing feed for goats. That sometimes extends to droughts or times of other unusual weather as well. Thankfully, goats will eat many kinds of hay. They have strong preferences for alfalfa, clover, or other *legume hays* over grass hay. It's wonderful if you grow and bale your own hay from your own land, but in the event you buy it, you'll need to evaluate the cost of various kinds of hay versus the relative nutritional value.

 DEFINITION

Legume hay is any hay made of plants that grow a seed-containing pod. Peas, beans, clover, peanuts, and cowpeas all fall in this category.

Be sure to test-run the hay with your goats before you bring home a bunch of it. Goats can be very picky about their cuisine. A full-size goat with some daytime browsing and a medium winter climate needs about a ton of good-quality hay per year. If you buy it before you try it, you might have a lot of uneaten hay left over.

What does good-quality hay look like? First of all it's green, not tan or brown. It will have enough moisture to hold together but not so much it'll go moldy in the middle. If the grass hay is brittle or the alfalfa leaves are breaking off the stems, the hay is too dry. Hay from previous years' harvests will lose some nutrition, but it might still be acceptable. If you're buying hay, be sure you find a seller and arrange for how much you want *well* before the need for it arises. Some feed stores carry hay year-round, but the quality will be variable and the cost higher than when getting it from the guy who grows it.

Hay needs to stay dry until the goat eats it, so be sure you have appropriate dry storage. In very wet climates, the best place is in a dry barn. In dryer climates, it may be a lean-to or even outdoors with a tarp covering. It's frustrating to buy good hay and go to the work of hauling and stacking it, only to have it damaged by wet weather.

GOAT HORN

Moldy hay is toxic and kills goats. Never feed hay that contains moldy spots!

If you want milk production, you want high-protein-content hay. And the better the quality and higher the protein content of the hay, the more milk your goats will produce. I've seen a dairy goat who was producing about 2½ quarts of milk a day increase her production to just under a gallon of milk per day when her diet was switched to high-protein, *third-cutting* alfalfa. With a high protein content (up to 22 percent), it's called dairy-quality hay for good reason—it produces milk! You simply cannot expect high production of either milk or kids from a goat who isn't getting optimal feed. Your hay provider can often tell you the protein content of his or her hay, and it's a good thing to know.

DEFINITION

If the conditions are right, alfalfa keeps growing after it's been cut. In some climates, an alfalfa field can be cut multiple times, with each cutting creating a finer stem and higher protein content of the hay. Goats love **third-cutting** (or fourth-cutting) hay because the stems are fine enough for them to eat the whole thing.

Any kind of hay can have a wide range of protein content, depending on when it's cut, how it's raked and baled, and what the weather is like during haying. Grass hay tends to be much lower in protein than legumes, but alfalfa cut and baled after it's flowered may have lower protein than grass hay cut and baled at the peak of nutrition.

Really good hay producers know this stuff. I'd be wary of one who didn't. After years of looking at hay, you can often tell by appearance the protein percentage. County extension agents are available if you have any questions your hay producer can't tell you.

Grain Supplements

Goats love grains, but they don't need much of them. If the rest of a goat's diet is adequate in amount and nutrients, grain isn't really a necessity. The goat world is full of people who believe grain is mandatory for goats, but it's not for nutrition! If you're milking your goat, a treat of some grains on the milking stand is a good way to get her to show up and stand still for the procedure. In addition, a goat who is putting milk in the bucket can certainly use a few extra calories, which grain supplies. Studies show that past a minimum—about 1½ to 2 pounds per milking—more grain does not mean more milk.

The grain ration for goats is usually *COB*, or corn, oats, and barley in some combination. Most feed stores make a mixture of these three grains they think is palatable to animals. The exact proportions aren't important because the nutritional content of all three grains are very similar. Their primary purpose is extra calories for the goat. Your goats will digest the COB better if it's rolled or crimped. Think what the oatmeal in your own kitchen looks like. That oat grain has been rolled. You can find this at the feed store already rolled or crimped. Most commercial grain rations already come this way.

> **DEFINITION**
>
> **COB** stands for a grain mixture of corn, oats, and barley. **Dairy ration** is any grain mixture a protein supplement has been added to.

By itself, COB is usually about 11 or 12 percent protein. Good dairy-quality alfalfa can run 18 to 22 percent protein. As you can see, the grain mixture doesn't add substantially to the protein for milk production. You can add protein supplements to the grain to make what's commonly called a *dairy ration*. Feed stores usually make their own mixture, and often more than one that's got a boosted protein content of about 16 percent. Remember, grain is for calories and treats to entice goats to do what you wish them to do.

One word of caution before you change feed types (browse, hay, grains) or the quantity of any of these: changes must be done *slowly*. Quick feed changes in type or amount can cause serious digestive and metabolic problems that can sometimes be fatal. To change feed type, begin with small amounts of the new feed until the goat has adapted. Big changes in feed amount, such as a big increase in something they like, can cause acidosis, which is also potentially fatal. Make feed changes *gradual*—always!

GOAT HORN

Always check the ingredients in any supplements you're thinking of feeding to your goats. Don't use any formulations that contain urea. It's used to boost protein for dairy cows, but it's toxic to goats!

Other Goat Treats

Goats appreciate other treats as well. Sunflower seeds are a favorite. You can feed up to about 1 cup per day, depending on the size of the goat. Sunflower seeds will slightly increase the butterfat content of milk, which often improves flavor as well as calories of the milk.

Peanuts are also a goat favorite. Prunes, raisins, or pieces of fresh or dried fruit can be real goat inducements, too. In general, goats are fond of sweet things. Some goats love bananas, but some don't. Some love oranges and the peels, but some don't. Try different produce from your garden or orchard to find out what *your* goats like. Don't overdo treats, though. In general, a handful of peanuts or a few pieces of fruit are plenty at one time.

Why give your goats treats?

- It keeps them bonded to you, the treat-giver, and coming to you when you call.

- If you need to give pills of some kind (more discussion of health and treatments in Chapter 7), they can be easily hidden within a piece of fruit or other treat.

- The treats are good for the goats as long as they're not overdone.

Everyone likes a little treat now and then, goats and humans alike. Don't overdo it, and you'll both be happy.

Salt and Minerals

All goats need salt, and nearly all salt is mixed with minerals. While cows do well with salt blocks, goats need loose, dry salt, not salt in blocks. They don't have a rough tongue like cows to lick enough salt from a block.

Goat mineral needs are important to understand. A complete mineral explanation is beyond the scope of this book, but there are four minerals that bear your consideration because they play such a large part in goat health:

- Zinc
- Copper
- Calcium
- Selenium

Zinc plays a big role in skin health, but in severe deficiencies, it also causes loss of body weight, stunted growth, hair loss, sluggishness, a hunchback gait, depressed appetite, and digestive and respiratory problems.

Copper is important in keeping skin, lungs, blood vessels, and muscles elastic; in development and structure of bone; hair pigmentation; reproduction; and parasite resistance. Those are no small parts of goat health, but copper's most important role is in keeping the immune system functioning well.

Diagnosing copper deficiency may be difficult because it can cause such a variety of ills. A goat who's sick might be a goat low in copper. A goat whose color is fading is *probably* low in copper. But a goat with a bald tail tip is certainly copper deficient and will probably be having a variety of health issues until the condition is corrected.

Copper-deficient animals are far more susceptible to parasite infestations as well. Deficiency is common in goats as well as many other ruminants in the Americas because there's a broadly pervasive copper deficiency in soils. Therefore, having a good supply of copper in mineral mixes is mandatory. Never use a sheep mineral mix because sheep don't need as much copper, so their minerals will be copper-deficient for goats. Use one formulated for cows or, better still, for goats. If your mineral mix is not preventing deficiency, give the goats copper boluses. See www.saanendoah.com/copper1.html for information about copper and boluses.

Without enough calcium, muscles don't contract and relax, the heart doesn't beat, nerves don't transmit impulses, and blood doesn't clot. Bones and teeth are made of calcium, and it works closely with phosphorus, magnesium, and other minerals. Goats put calcium into the milk they produce as well as the bones of developing fetuses, so their demand for calcium is high.

Calcium deficiencies often show up at kidding time or when a goat is dealing with the early demands of heavy milk production. (More about calcium in Chapter 8.)

If you live in a selenium-deficient area, supplemental selenium is mandatory. Deficiencies cause white muscle disease that kills newborns, or if they survive, they'll be unthrifty and fail to thrive due to cardiac damage. There's no treatment for the young, but prevention is a simple selenium injection for the does before breeding or kidding. BoSe or MuSe is the shot to give. If your herd is copper-deficient, the body won't be able to absorb selenium efficiently. BoSe and MuSe can only be prescribed by a vet.

HERD HINTS

Check out cspinet.org/nah/selen.html or tin.er.usgs.gov/geochem/doc/averages/ se/usa.html for maps and other information about selenium levels in your area. As you'll see, there's not complete agreement between sources, so be sure to check with your veterinarian.

All these minerals and several others are needed in a certain proportion to each other. Depending on the minerals in the soil where your goats range plus the mineral content of their hay and supplements, you absolutely will need to supply a mineral mix to meet the demand.

Copper is low in most soils, and therefore low in feeds and forages as well. The availability of zinc and copper can be affected by other things such as iron in the water or molybdenum levels in alfalfa. Calcium is low in grass, grass hay, and grains. Calcium is much higher in alfalfa and other legume hays. For selenium, check with your veterinarian.

I give you this brief introduction to goat minerals, not to make it crystal clear, but rather to illustrate that the subject is complex. For your own goats, be sure you're providing a good mineral mix based on what forages and hay they eat.

Check the mixes at your local feed stores. Several goat-supply businesses make mineral mixes specifically for goats. (See Appendix B for a list of suppliers.) Always look for mixes high in copper and low in salt (salt should be available separately), and check for palatability. If your goats don't like the taste, they won't eat it and it does them no good. If your goats graze on pastures and eat grass hay in the winter months, your mineral mix should have a higher ratio of calcium to phosphorus than if they browse or eat alfalfa hay.

Also check with people already raising goats in your area, particularly those with very healthy goats. They should be able to help you choose a good mineral mix that's right for your goats and your area.

Why worry about minerals? It may be possible for goats to get a balanced diet, including minerals, if they live as nature originally designed them to do. Under those circumstances, the demands were fewer and less rigorous. The goats you have (or will soon get) have been modified for specific purposes. They're kept in circumstances that put different stresses on their nutritional needs. Like humans, a goat's health depends on her lifestyle and diet. If you climb mountains in the Himalayas, your nutritional needs will be greater than if you sit at a desk all day. Goats asked to produce milk or meat or fiber all year long are the mountain climbers of the goat species. Paying attention to their minerals is insurance to keep them healthy and productive. Prevention rather than cure!

Water

Milk is about 93 percent water. Bodies are about 65 percent water. Ensuring an adequate supply of clean drinking water for your goats is *mandatory*.

Be sure to place water buckets, tubs, or tanks high enough so the goat berries (fecal matter) don't contaminate the water. Water with manure in it smells and tastes unpleasant, to say the least. Would you want to drink that? Neither will your goats, which means they're unlikely to drink enough.

Even worse, contaminated water means parasite eggs from the fecal matter get into their water, compounding any parasite problem. (More about parasites in Chapter 7.)

That Goat's Got Personality!

People-friendly goats can be a lot of fun because they're usually where you are, even if that means they're sometimes a little intrusive, too. Friendly goats are certainly easier to care for. Wild or standoffish goats are less companionable, less in-your-face, but a lot harder to care for because you must catch them before any intervention (medications, milking, shearing, hoof trimming, preparing for births, etc.). Before you bring goats onto your farm, you need to be very clear about what purpose they serve.

Wild goats may be perfect for brush cleanup. However, tame, friendly goats would be equally suitable. I have a bias for goats who like me and enjoy my company. But not everyone does.

If a kid is bottle-raised, she will be bonded with her new "mother"—you—and will forever be oriented toward people. If you plan to milk your goats, tame ones will make your life easier. They're more fun because they will interact with you. As mentioned in Chapter 1, one of the advantages of goats over other livestock is their companionability, most of which is lost if they're dam-raised.

KIDDING AROUND

How a goat is raised determines almost the entirety of her people orientation. If a kid goat is raised by her mother, she will be bonded to goats and not people. Depending on how much, if any, handling she gets by people, she may simply run away at the mere sight of you.

A dam-raised kid is bonded to her mother and might be very skittish around people, including you.

When you're searching for goats to buy, be sure to consider their tameness or lack of it. When you're raising your own goat offspring, you need to decide whether to bottle-raise the babies or let Mom do it. The following table offers an at-a-glance list of the pros and cons of bottle- versus dam-raised goats.

Before babies arrive at your farm, think about which method meets your needs best. If you decide to bottle-raise, of course, you need to acquire the supplies ahead of your kid arrivals. That includes nipples (there are several kinds), bottles (usually pop bottles will do), and milking supplies. (More on milking equipment and supplies in Chapter 9.)

A bottle-raised kid is bonded to humans.
(Nathaniel Kemper)

Methods of Raising Kids

Dam-Raised Kids	Bottle-Raised Kids
Standoffish or wild	Bonded to people
Harder to catch	Sometimes too friendly
It's easy, no work	It's a lot of work
It's nature's method	You're available 24/7
With multiples, milk may be scarce	Ensures enough milk

What About Tethering?

Now that you know a lot more about the nature of a goat, how they prefer to navigate for food, and how they are a social, herd animal, you can probably understand why it's completely against their nature to be tied on a rope. They cannot wander and eat where they prefer. They are isolated from companions. They are quite likely to get tangled in the rope. They are likely to knock over the water bucket and end up thirsty. They are often unable to get to shade as needed or get out of the rain. A goat on a rope is an invitation to predators (including neighboring dogs) to come get a free meal.

There are probably some occasions when tethering is an easy solution, and they usually revolve around not having fences in a particular brushy or grassy spot. Please, exercise a little more effort. You can build your own temporary fences using metal fence panels, as described in Chapter 2.

If you don't have the fences to manage goats, that may be where you should start, rather than tethering a goat, which is going to be a very unsatisfactory experience for the goat … and probably for you, too.

The Least You Need to Know

- Understanding the personality and nature of goats gives you knowledge about what to expect and what to do.
- Goat food preferences are quite specific, and it's in both your and your goats' best interests to accommodate those preferences as much as possible.
- Supplemental feed such as grain isn't so much for nutrition as it is for enticing goats to your agenda, such as getting on the milk stand. It's a treat!
- Friendly goats are more fun than wild goats, and you can influence that by how you raise the babies.
- Tethering goats is not a happy solution to a lack of fencing.

Caring for Your Goats

In This Chapter

- Maintaining your goats
- What to do about horns, neutering, identification, and hair clipping
- Another look at equipment

I won't lie to you: goat care isn't always fun, and it isn't always pretty. But it's still necessary. Some of the procedures I discuss in this chapter are decidedly unpleasant. You've heard the saying, "A stitch in time saves nine"? Remember that saying when we look at some of those unpleasant chores, and keep in mind that if these tasks were ignored, things could get ugly.

Some goat care is fairly simple, but some requires developing basic skills you might not currently have. The goal of this book is to help you develop those skills, so both you and your goats have the best experience possible. Some of the things we cover may save you from disaster. Some help you create a better outcome. All of them ultimately make the well-managed goat operation more pleasant and productive for all parties.

Hoof Care

All goats have hooves, and those hooves are always growing, much like your own fingernails. The goat foot has two toes, making them part of the group of cloven-hoofed animals, along with cows, sheep, deer, and pigs. The foot structure has a hard outer covering called the *hoof wall*. Inside that, on each toe, is the *sole*, a softer tissue that helps provide traction and padding. The reason goats can climb so well is, in part, because of the nature of that sole. On newborns, the hoof structure is gelatinous, and normally, parts peel away within minutes of birth as the outer wall hardens.

The Importance of Keeping Things Trimmed

Imagine your toenails growing over the ends of your toes and curling into strange shapes. That's similar to what happens to goat hooves, except the goats have to walk on the curled, overgrown part. In addition, the hoof wall can cover the sole, changing the goat's ability to stick to the things they want to climb. Overgrown hooves tend to extend toward the front of the hoof because the toes grow faster than the heels. This gives the foot the appearance of long-toed medieval jester shoes. That forward extension of the toes changes the mechanics of the foot, putting huge stresses on the pastern and structures of the foot.

> **KIDDING AROUND**
>
> In the wild, goats wear away the hoof wall and sole about as fast as it grows by running around on mountains and rocks. As soon as goats start living on pastures and the softer terrain of woodlands and feedlots, the hoof very quickly grows faster than any wear keeps it worn down.

Overgrown feet are uncomfortable for the goat. If left untreated, as the hoof wall closes over the sole, it traps manure and moisture, a prescription for infection. One potential problem is hoof rot. Another is having a goat end up "down on her pasterns." Other foot and leg problems can result in lameness and less-productive goats. After all, if their feet hurt, the goats aren't going to eat well, drink enough water, or carry kids or a full udder as productively as they otherwise could.

To avoid problems, goat feet need to be trimmed in most domesticated situations. Dairy goats need trimming at least every six weeks, some meat goat operations go much longer than that, but the frequency really depends on your goats, how they are fed, and the terrain they have to walk on. Check your goats' feet every four weeks until you figure out how often you need to trim their feet to keep them happy and healthy.

Hoof Maintenance Tools and Techniques

Many tools can be used for trimming hooves. Some people use a pocket knife. Others use a linoleum knife. (Use caution with these—if the goat jerks away, you may need stitches in your hand or leg!) Most experienced breeders, however, favor handheld pruners. This tool is small enough for most hands, including women's and most teenagers', to use comfortably. It's versatile enough to get the job done, and it's easy to sharpen when needed. In addition, pruners are relatively inexpensive, usually well under $20.

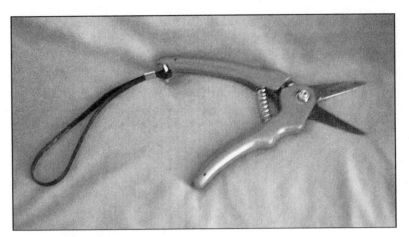

Pruners like these are a great tool for trimming goat hooves.

To trim your goat's hooves, you must start by restraining the goat. I prefer getting her up off the ground because it's easier on your back, but many people restrain them at ground level. Face the goat from the front and off to her side a little. Pick up her front foot, gently turning it so you can see the bottom of the hoof. Start by cutting away the overgrown hoof wall. Trim each side, and clean out any dirt as you go. The softer center of her toes may have some extra growth, too, particularly on the heel and in between the heels. Flatten and smooth those little tabs of extra tissue. You can get the surface nice and flat by cutting or by filing. The goat might object more to filing than cutting, and it really isn't needed.

These feet show the extra hoof growth that needs to be trimmed off.
(Veralyn Srch-Harelson)

If your goat's feet are overgrown and the toe is longer, shorten that. Badly overgrown feet almost always have longer toes that change the correct mechanics of the goat's foot and leg. To shorten the toe section correctly, set her foot back on a level surface and look for the horizontal growth rings around her hoof. If needed, clean it with water and a brush until you can see the growth lines. (They're similar to the growth rings in a tree.) The bottom of the trimmed hoof should be parallel to the growth rings. That probably means you need to trim more off just the toe section of the foot. Be careful to only cut a little at a time. Watch for the "pink." Cutting beyond the pink leads to bleeding that's both painful for the goat and could allow for infection.

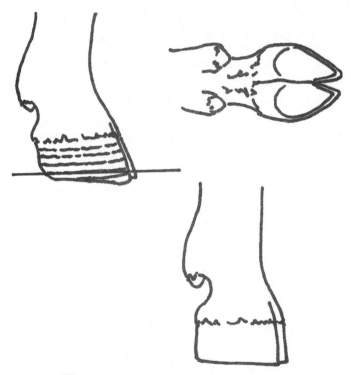

These examples show a correctly trimmed foot.
(Veralyn Srch-Harelson)

If you can watch someone trim feet before you do it, it will give you some confidence. Many websites show pictures and even videos of hoof trimming. Just Google "goat hoof trimming" or search YouTube to find some of these websites.

GOAT HORN

Always wear leather gloves when trimming goat feet, especially on the hand holding the foot, to protect your hands in case the goat jerks. I've seen some very nasty cuts on unprotected hands. Heavy denim jeans or chaps will protect your legs.

If you'd like to extend the time between hoof trimming, try building the goats a climbing toy or goat jungle gym with a rough surface that will help grind down their hooves. Use building materials that have a gritty surface like roofing tiles, stair tread covers, or just a covering of rough concrete. I guarantee they'll climb on it (goats climb on *everything!*) and the rough surface will help wear down their feet the natural way, extending the time between when you need to trim. Large chunks of concrete from torn-down buildings work great, too. They're just hard to move!

The Great Horn Debate

A few subjects within the goat world stir up great controversy. Whether or not to have horns on your goats is one of those subjects. Ultimately, the decision is up to you, but let's look at both sides of the controversy.

Some goats naturally grow no horns; these are called *polled* goats. For a baby to be polled, it must have one polled parent. Polled goats survive just as well as horned goats so it's unlikely that horns have any survival value, at least in domesticity.

Horn Pros and Cons

Some people say horns are a protection against predators. They may be, but many horned goats are still killed by dogs and other predators, so I'm suspicious about their usefulness as protection. Some people like the look of horns. That's a legitimate preference. Some people like horns as a way to control and maneuver goats—a handle of sorts.

Some people claim keeping horns on goats helps disperse heat in a hot climate. Much literature cites this as a common fact, but there doesn't seem to be any research to back it up as physiologic fact. If it is true, then the reverse would also be true, that horns disperse heat in cold weather when heat dispersal is a drain on the goat's resources. I can't verify that heat dispersal through horns is actual or that it would make a difference in any significant way.

Horns do have some downsides. Goats use their horns to boss each other around. The tips of horns get very sharp and pointy, and those pointy tips can inflict damage. Even very tame goats who are friendly to their people can jerk their heads and inadvertently do some damage, ranging from mild pokes or scratches to severe stab injuries and eye wounds. Children are even more at risk around horned goats for the simple fact that they're at a level closer to the horns. Horn injuries can be serious.

Once in a while, a poorly adjusted goat with horns (often a male) will take it upon himself to demolish walls, fences, or whole buildings by repeatedly hitting it with his horns. (Goats are incredibly effective battering rams!) It's impossible to thwart a persistent animal set on breaking down barriers with his horns. It's quite possible that he'll destroy a fence or small building in a short amount of time.

Another downside of horns is that in 4-H, FFA, and all dairy-goat-sanctioned shows, horns are not permitted. This may not be true of all meat goat shows; some allow horns and some do not.

The biggest downfall I see with horned goats is that they tend to get stuck. Goats are notoriously curious and investigative. They love to stick their heads through openings so small you'd swear they couldn't possibly fit. Horns can get through, too, but then they can't get back out, especially through fences like woven wire, welded wire, and some electric fencing types. Then you've got a goat stuck in the most vulnerable of positions. Horror stories abound of goats eaten by predators, having a heat stroke, or dying of dehydration in such situations. Also, if a goat stands up on his hind legs and puts his head through a fence and, heaven forbid, slips, the goat will strangle slowly or have a broken neck.

I've had goats with horns, and I've had goats without. My preference is for no horns. My experience is primarily with dairy breeds where it's a given that goats will be hornless. You must decide for your own operation. Make up your mind early on whether you'll have horned or hornless goats because the time to decide is virtually the moment the babies hit the ground.

Removing Goat Horns

There are two ways to get rid of horns, and neither is pleasant. The easiest way is to *disbud* the newborns by cutting off the blood supply to the horns. Depending on the breed of goat, some are born with bumps that clearly show the start of horns. Some breeds will take 10 days or 2 weeks for those buds to appear. *Dehorning* is far less pleasant. The horn must be surgically sawed off at the base of the skull. It leaves the goat's upper sinuses open, requiring care to avoid debris getting into them or fly problems. I find dehorning barbaric and abhorrent.

DEFINITION

To **disbud** is to stop horns from growing, usually by cauterizing the blood supply to horn tissue. To **dehorn** is to cut horns off an adult goat with a surgical saw. **Scurs** are partial horn growth that can curl back into the goat's head or neck.

If you decide to disbud the kids to prevent horns, you'll benefit from watching it done by an expert first. It must be done before the small buds develop too much. That's almost always within two weeks of birth and for some it's within days of birth.

For disbudding, you'll need a disbudding iron, available commercially from goat supply businesses listed in Appendix B. This isn't a place to scrimp on cost. Get the best iron you can afford. The hotter the iron, the shorter the time you have to leave it on the goat's head. Breeders sometimes use iron pipe heated with a blowtorch to disbud. Just remember, the iron must be *red hot* to be effective.

You may want to clip the hair over the horn bud. That keeps the disbudding tool from burning through the hair before it reaches skin. To do this, first restrain the kid. Place the hot iron over the bud for no more than 10 seconds at a time. Look for a copper-colored ring around the horn bud. When you see that copper ring, you're done. If you don't adequately restrain the kid, burns to both you and the kid could result.

Disbudding a kid's horns keeps her horns from growing.
(Nathaniel Kemper)

During the disbudding procedure, the iron needs to cauterize all the blood vessels feeding the horn tissue. Be tough, and burn long enough to do that. Some people also rotate the iron against the goat's head to ensure it works thoroughly. It's difficult to deliberately inflict pain on a cute little goat. But don't let your feelings keep you from doing an adequate job. The consequences could be far worse for the goat than the initial disbudding when the horns—or worse yet, *scurs*—begin growing and it has to be done a second time.

If you burn for too long, however, you might cause brain swelling. Cool that head quickly to reduce the kid's pain.

> **HERD HINT**
>
> So the goat has made a racket and you feel terribly guilty and positively awful. Here's your chance to atone. The disbudding caused a burn, and what makes burns feel better? Ice water. Have a bucket of ice water handy with a ladle or other utensil to drizzle cold water over the burned spots. It will make both of you feel better. If you're bottle-raising these babies, have a bottle ready, too. No baby goat can remember pain for long when a bottle is offered!

A caustic paste is available to spread on the goat's horn buds. It chemically burns just as the iron does with heat. The paste is very dangerous, though. It often gets into the goats' eyes and causes blindness, or it gets rubbed off onto other goats, causing serious burns or blindness. *Never* use it!

Minding the Males: Neutering

Male goats make up half the number of kids born, statistically speaking. But having more male goats than you need for breeding purposes is simply not fun or practical. They're obnoxious in some of their habits, behaviors, and scent. They do not make good pets. They're larger, stronger, and far more aggressive than the females. Like all mature male livestock, they are harder to manage than females. Handling the buck(s) you need for breeding is mandatory, but extra males simply complicate life.

But here they are! All those little bucks will grow up into big bucks. This is where you need to make another tough decision. What are you going to do with the extra goats you produce, especially the extra males? Your choices are:

- Dispatch (kill) them at birth
- Raise to weaning for meat for your family

- Raise for meat and take them to an auction or sell to buyers

- Try to sell them as pets or pack/cart animals

Please don't give away unneutered males as pets. They are only cute for a few months, and then they almost always turn into huge problems.

If you're raising your own meat and will butcher at 3 to 5 months of age, neutering may not be necessary. Some breeds reach puberty before 3 months so be sure no females are at risk of unplanned breedings. If you will raise them longer, neutering is mandatory.

GOAT HORN

Some of the miniature breeds can breed at about 7 weeks, both males and females, so the extra males must be neutered younger.

The neutered male goat is called a *wether*, just as a neutered bull is called a steer. Wethers don't develop the buck behaviors or smell and can easily live with the females. Neutered male goats make good pets and can be great pack or cart goats.

When you've made the decision to neuter, your next decision is which method you want to use:

- Surgical castration

- Banding

- Burdizzoing

Again, while this procedure is not fun to do, it prevents untold difficulty and misery down the road.

Some farmers know how to do surgical castration; some take the animals to a veterinarian. I don't like surgical castration. I've seen two animals bleed to death from this kind of neutering, one done by a vet and one done by a farmer, so it's not my choice. Get training from someone who knows what they're doing if you choose this method.

Banding requires a tool that stretches a small rubber band around the testicles at the body wall, cutting off the blood supply to the testicles, which then wither and drop off in a matter of weeks. The goat experiences some discomfort for a while, but it's short-lived. Use caution so that no other tissues (such as teats) get stuck in the band. Also, keep a close eye on the goat because infection can result with banding. Many breeders simply cut off the tissue below the band after about five to seven days, reducing the potential for infection. Be certain the goat is protected from tetanus infection by giving the CDT vaccination. See more about vaccinations in Chapter 7.

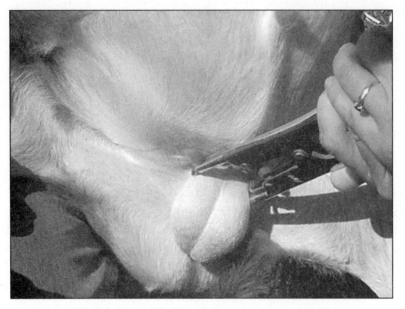

The banding method is one way to neuter male kids.
(Nathaniel Kemper)

The burdizzo is a clamplike tool used to crush the blood vessels going to the testicles. When the blood supply is interrupted, it causes testicle necrosis, similar to the banding method. I've never seen this method done so I can't report firsthand knowledge, but I've heard it's supposed to lower the risk of bleeding and infection. This method requires experience, and the tool is more expensive than the banding tool.

Proving Who's Who: Tattooing

If you buy registered goats, they must be tattooed for identification. The goats with ears get a unique-to-the-farm tattoo in each ear. Goats with tiny or no external ears (LaManchas) get a tattoo in the web or center of their tail. That's how the registry organization recognizes their parentage and verifies your goats are who you say they are.

Even if your goats aren't registered, you may want to consider tattoos for your own record-keeping and identification. This may be especially important if your goats are a breed where they all look pretty much alike.

If you decide you want your goats identified with tattoos, you must have, or have access to, a tattoo kit. It consists of a type of pliers with flat surfaces that come together on each side of an ear (or tail). One side of the tool has tattoo digits that make small holes in the flesh in the shape of the tattoo you've chosen. Then you rub tattoo ink into the holes and they heal over with color. The colored scars become the tattoo.

GOAT HORN

Be careful not to hit any blood vessels when tattooing your goats! In the goat's ear, there's a space between the major blood vessels where the tattoo should go. Tattooing the tail is the same except the tissue is fleshier and the blood vessels aren't as prominent.

Most tattoo kits come with a container of black paste ink. If your goats have white skin, that's perfect. Most goats have dark skin, though, and the black ink is hard or impossible to read. In these cases, use green ink because it will show up on all skin colors. It will probably be a separate purchase.

Tattoo kits come in several sizes, and the one you use depends on the size of goat you're tattooing. Check with others with your breed of goat to see what they use.

Tattooing a goat too young often makes the tattoo unreadable in the adult. As the kid's ear grows, the colored dots spread, but not always in a way to make them decipherable. If you tattoo the kids when they're a little older (3 to 5 months), their ears have done much of their growing. The downside is that they're harder to handle.

Another misstep that can make adult tattoos unreadable is if you don't squeeze the tongs together enough and some of the little holes of the numbers or letters aren't completely made in the ear.

If you don't clean the ear before tattooing, the oils and dirt in the ear can keep the ink from getting into the holes, and the tattoo will be unreadable.

After you've made the holes for the tattoo, you must rub the ink thoroughly into them. Some people use an old, soft toothbrush they have disinfected or just their fingers. Either way, wear gloves, or your hands will be stained for many days after! If the holes are bleeding or seeping, use a paper towel to blot and continue to rub ink into the holes until the bleeding has stopped. The bleeding washes out the ink, and you'll end up with an unreadable tattoo. An optional step after the tattoo is well inked, is to cover the area with baking soda.

This goat is getting a tattoo in her ear.
(Nathaniel Kemper)

As with any of the care procedures, it really helps if you can see it done by an expert with lots of practice before you do it on your own.

Most of the meat goat breeds use an ear tag for identification rather than a tattoo. It's an option for any breed unless you plan to show them at some point. Ear tags have potential for getting ripped out of the ear and leaving an unsightly ear injury.

To Clip or Not to Clip?

Fiber goats definitely need to be sheared, or clipped, to harvest their fiber. But what about nonfiber goats? Do they get clipped or not?

The answer is maybe. If you have dairy goats and plan to show them, traditionally they should be clipped before showing. It's not a hard-and-fast rule, though, and you'll sometimes see goats in the show ring with longer hair—but not often. Meat goats are usually clipped to show. It depends on the local show rules, so check with the officials before you get out your clippers.

The Pros and Cons of Clipping

Many breeds of goats get pretty hairy—some with *very* long hair. They seem to appreciate getting a haircut at least once a year to get rid of the itches and dandruff that accumulate. For the owner, it's a good way to assess your goats for thinness, fatness, conformation, and other health details—for instance, do they have lice or ticks or other external parasites?

There's another really good reason for clipping milk goats, at least partially. If you plan to milk her, think about the mechanics of long goat hair around her belly and udder. She lies down in dirt and manure, and some of it stays in the long hair. Dirt and manure are bursting with bacteria. When you milk her, you put your milk bucket under her, and with every movement some of the dirt and manure is falling into your bucket to contaminate the milk. I talk more about milk sanitation in Chapter 8, but for now, consider that if all that long hair around the underside of the udder is clipped off, your milk will be much cleaner, and therefore more wholesome for your family.

Clipping Tips and Techniques

The partial clip for cleanliness of the milk is called the *dairy clip*. Starting at the udder and clipping against the direction the hair grows, clip toward the front legs to approximately the middle of the belly. Clip up the back of the leg toward the tail because that area also is roughly above your milk bucket. Always clip against the direction the hair grows, and be observant because the direction changes at bends and cowlicks.

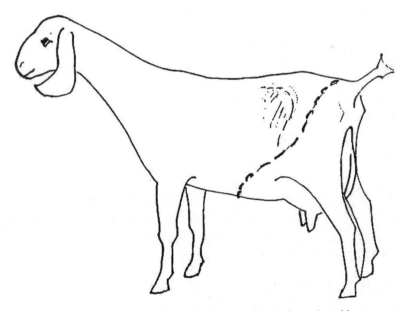

For a dairy clip, remove the hair around and above the udder.

If you're going to do any clipping or shearing, you may want to invest in two sets of clippers. The large animal clipper is good for the main parts of the body, and with the right blades, it's also good for shearing. The A-5 type of clipper is smaller, lighter, and better around heads, udders, and legs. Both kinds are available at goat supply houses. Even the best clippers get hot with extended use, so be sure you keep up the maintenance and oiling. If you decide to clip goats, you will need extra blades in different sizes, depending on how short you're clipping. You also need to line up a blade-sharpening person or shop because the blades do get dull with use.

GOAT HORN

A newly sheared goat, especially those with light skin, can suffer extreme sunburn. Keep her inside, covered, or sprinkle her with lots of baby powder, white flour, or dust for a little while as her newly exposed skin acclimatizes.

Preventing Bad Habits

From the day goats are born, they tend to behave as goats do. One of the main behaviors is butting. It's natural for them. Unfortunately, while it's very cute to see a little goat playing at butting, it must *not* be encouraged. Too many people play with their goat kids pretending to butt them. What's cute in a newborn becomes dangerous behavior in an adult who thinks she's *supposed* to butt people. Goats who butt people are unacceptable. But remember, it's not all on the goats; it's what their people have encouraged them to do.

As mentioned earlier, probably the best goat-training tool is the spray bottle filled with water. Goats hate to get wet, so a quick spray in the face is a good way to discourage a behavior. For goats who jump up on people or look like they might be thinking of butting (they tip their heads slightly to the side and raise their front quarters), a quick spray of water to the face helps change their mind.

In Chapter 10, we look at training goats for more specialized purposes, but for now, just remember that bad behaviors should be discouraged right from the start. It is *not* okay for goats to jump on or butt people—ever!

Other Goat-Care Equipment

There are a few other things you'll need for caring for your goats. Planning for these ahead of the need for them will make your goat experience go more smoothly.

Feeding Equipment

For two or three goats, feeding can be fairly simple. They need some kind of manger for hay and buckets or a feed box of some kind for grain, treats, salt, and minerals. A bucket or tub for water rounds out the feeding equipment.

Keeping feed up off the ground is a good idea. Keeping goat feet out of the feed pays big dividends in parasite management. Goats are notorious for wasting hay. Many a goat-raiser has tried to design a manger their goats can eat from but can't pull hay out to waste. I have yet to see one that is perfect!

The simplest I've ever seen is just a tub with hay in it. If it's on the ground, eventually some goat will stand in it or use it as a bed. But setting it up on a platform can be a good solution. Many setups have hay fed on the outside of a cattle panel fence. The goats must stick their heads through and the fence prevents them from contaminating the hay. One farm I visited left bales of hay just at the outside of the fence, strings or wires intact, so the goats had to work to get hay loose from the bale. The fence was made of cattle panels, so the goats (without horns, of course) could put their heads through.

 GOAT HORN

Leaving strings on bales of hay might have a serious downside. If a goat swallows a plastic baling string, a serious digestive problem, or possibly death, may result!

You can build mangers out of cattle panel pieces with a box interior for hay, and many goats can eat from it at once. There are a million designs. Visit several goat operations so you can see how others are doing it. Review the drawings and information in Chapter 2, too.

Milking Equipment

If you want to milk goats, you need a milk stand. The purpose is partly to restrain the goat, but mostly to make it comfortable and easy for you to get good, clean milk.

If the goat is at ground level, you'll be uncomfortable. Milk stands can be at a height for you to sit or stand at, depending on your preference. It can be wide enough for you to sit on the edge, or it might have a built-in seat. Or you might prefer an independent chair. It needs a head stanchion to lock the goat's head in place, and it needs a container for her grain ration.

Consider if you want it against a wall or open on both sides. I like one against the wall because it further restricts the goat's movements. The open-on-both-sides model is nice for trimming feet. You can freely move to the other side to do the other two feet more easily.

Deciding on the size of your milk stand and the other details depends on your goats. Are they full-size dairy goats or miniatures? Are they a wide-bodied meat breed? Are they obstreperous and difficult to control or placid and eager for milking? Are they young and able to jump up on a platform, or do they need a ramp to get there? Now how about you? How tall are you? Do you have any aches and pains that need consideration? The answers will determine the details of what will work for you. Design it to your own preferences.

Next, you need a simple brush to brush her belly and around her udder to remove debris and dust. A hair brush is fine; you don't have to buy a special kind of livestock brush. Just be sure it's not so stiff that it hurts the goat, or so soft it fails to do the job of brushing her underside clean of debris.

Now let's talk about the milk bucket. There are those who claim only stainless steel will do. It's probably best because it's easy to keep scrupulously clean. Many people use food-grade plastic milk buckets. An emptied ice-cream bucket may work, too, or any bucket that used to have food in it. Plastic can absorb food odors and material, possibly growing bacteria, so be careful with plastic. Clean it in your dishwasher or use automatic dishwashing powder to clean it. Soak it in that solution overnight a couple times a week. Plastic is an inexpensive alternative to stainless steel, but only if you're careful.

No matter how careful you are in milking your goat, some debris will fall into the bucket. That debris carries bacteria, which are now in the milk. It's important to strain the milk immediately to minimize bacteria that grow in the milk.

To strain milk, use a milk filter. These circles of porous material fit in the filter funnels available at goat supply houses and catch all the hair and debris picked up during milking. If you don't want to invest in the filter funnel, the milk filter can be fitted into a regular funnel placed in the mouth of the jar your milk will be stored in.

Glass is great for milk storage, and Kerr, Mason, and other brands make canning jars (with lids) in many sizes. Other glass is suitable, too.

With very little investment in equipment, you could be enjoying fresh, wholesome, delicious milk from your own goats.

These are some of the items you'll need for milking.
(Nathaniel Kemper)

Health Equipment

Prevention is always better than treatment. But in the event that some of your goats don't look or feel right, you need a few things on hand to care for them.

Be sure you have a thermometer. I like a glass one, while other breeders use plastic or digital. Use it rectally. Shake down the thermometer so it's below 96 or 97 degrees Fahrenheit, insert it with a little lubricant or, in a pinch, just a little cool water. Leave it in for five minutes, remove, and then read the temperature. A goat's normal temperature is 102°F, although, depending on the weather, it can be as high as 103°F and still be "normal." Before you can decide what to do with a sick goat, you *must* know her temperature. (I talk more about sick goats in Chapter 8.)

HERD HINT

Taking a sick goat to the veterinarian is expensive. And worse, many veterinarians have little or no goat experience, so you should always ask! With some practice, you can learn to treat many of common goat ailments yourself.

You'll also need a supply of syringes and needles and a proper disposal container (called a Sharps container) for both. Syringes in 3-, 6-, and 12-milliliter sizes will cover most of your needs. The larger sizes are sometimes used for giving oral medications that use larger doses. Needles come in sizes called *gauges*. An 18-, 20-, or 22-gauge needle is suitable for most goat medicines. The larger number is the smaller needle and won't work for viscous medicines.

Discuss with your veterinarian what medicines he or she thinks are appropriate for you to keep on hand. I like to keep some general antibiotic, anthelminetics (wormers), and a few vaccinations on hand, but decide with your medical practitioner what's best for you.

Collars

Most people find it's handy to have collars on their goats. It gives you a convenient way to lead them where you want them and control them during clipping, tattooing, or many other types of care.

Collars might be as controversial as horns, though, and there are lots of ideas out there. Your decision depends, in part, on how your goats live. If they browse over many acres in terrain with lots of brush and shrubbery, a snug, unbreakable collar could get caught on something and very quickly strangle the goat. For that situation, I prefer breakaway plastic chain collars. They're durable enough for manipulating the goat by the collar, but if she gets snagged and jerks hard against it, it will break and she won't strangle. (Breakaway dog collars work well for goats.)

If you have horned goats, another danger is that one goat will get her horn caught in another goat's collar, causing strangulation.

In a small pen with no snags to worry about, metal or woven fabric collars may be perfectly suitable. The collar should always be loose enough so if the collar gets snagged, the goat can get loose by slipping out of it.

KIDDING AROUND

Leashes are sometimes used on the miniature goats to minimize bending down to their level. They are never used on dairy goats. A leash does not give you much control over a goat unless she's a very agreeable goat, and few are. They are most often seen on miniature goats so their handlers don't have to bend over.

Before you decide on collars, examine the conditions where your goats live so you can be sure their collars are safe and still give you the control you need. Collars need not be expensive—even your local dollar store can be a good place to shop!

There are many other things you *could* keep on hand, but for now, these are the basics to help you deal with goat health—both treatment and prevention.

The Least You Need to Know

- Learn how to trim your goats' feet for comfort and soundness.
- Do you want horned or hornless goats? There are pros and cons for each, so make the best decision for you and your goats.
- You have to decide what to do about the extra males born at your farm and learn castrating techniques.
- Preventing bad habits from getting a foothold helps make the experience better for everyone—goats and humans.
- You don't need a ton of specialized tools to raise goats, but some basic equipment will help you better manage your animals.

Goat Reproduction

In This Chapter

- What to expect with male goats
- Details of the breeding season
- Handling pregnancy and birth
- The care and development of kids

Goats are mammals, and all mammals produce milk to feed their young. It's not an automatic thing when they reach adulthood, but rather a part of their reproductive cycle. In order to produce milk, goats must first produce young.

Goat reproduction has some similarities to reproduction in other livestock, so if you have other livestock experience, that will help. If not, this chapter gives you enough basics to give you some confidence.

Mastering the Males

Let's start with the males because they're necessary, obviously. But male goats can be pretty surprising if you have no experience with them.

Sexual maturity usually starts before 6 months but can begin earlier in some breeds and later in some others. I once had a 7-month-old Nigerian Dwarf doe give birth to a perfectly healthy single kid, although it was a difficult birth. Backtracking, it seems she was bred at 7 weeks of age. On the other hand, I've seen some Nubian bucks who weren't mature enough for breeding until 8 or 9 months.

At sexual maturity, male goats have a strong odor. Most people don't care for it, but the lady goats do—such is the nature of Mother Nature. The buck smell will be all over his body but is strongest near his scent glands on the top of his head. If you get the scent on you, it's extremely hard to remove and requires much soap and scrubbing. Avoid touching stinky bucks if you can't stand the smell. Orange-based hand cleaners seem to easily remove buck odor. Many of these are automotive-type hand cleaners.

The male goat in *rut* urinates on himself, often spraying his front legs and face with urine. He will also urinate into his mouth and then curl his upper lip as if to get a good take on his own scent. The combination of these behaviors—which are normal, by the way—coats his hair around the front of his body and head with a sticky, smelly layer that's part of his appeal to the ladies, even if not to his caretakers. He's not always selective in his spraying, either, and might spray humans and other nongoat species, or even attempt mounting. He also gets frequent erections, which he checks out with his mouth.

> **DEFINITION**
>
> **Rut** is the period of heightened sexual activity during breeding season common to all mammals with a defined breeding season.

Bucks also engage in blubbering and tongue flapping. He may lower his head and flap his tongue at objects of his affection. Blubbering is hard to describe, but when you hear it, you'll know right away!

These are all sexual behaviors geared toward getting the female "in the mood." They may appear singly or in combination. Keep in mind that the male goat isn't picky. He'll use these tricks indiscriminately on all other goats, people, or other species within his reach!

Once you're aware of bucks' normal behavior, it's easy to see why you wouldn't necessarily want to have more bucks than you need. Some people choose not to have a buck at all and take their females to a buck at another farm for breeding. That option isn't always available, though, and comes with some plusses and minuses.

When breeding season is over, some of these behaviors diminish a little, especially in young bucks. Some older ones never really go out of rut and may continue the mating behaviors all year round.

The Breeding Season and Heat Cycles

The full-size dairy goat breeds—those originating in European areas—have a discrete breeding season. It usually begins in late August or September and goes through January. During those months, these goats are able to become pregnant. The miniatures—those who originated in Africa—and some of the meat goat breeds have a less-defined breeding season and will breed during most of the year.

For dairy breeds, this means most milk goats will have a dry period (usually 60 days) before they have their new kids during the late winter and spring months. For breeds with a longer breeding season, the dry months can be staggered to ensure a continuous supply of fresh milk. The traditional winter dry period, however, can be a small vacation from the unrelenting nature of milking twice a day.

Female goats reach sexual maturity at different ages. The Nigerian I mentioned earlier in this chapter was exceptionally on the young side. Most dairy breeds start heat cycles anytime past about 5 or 6 months of age, depending on their birth date.

When they're old enough to breed depends more on their early nutrition than an actual date of sexual maturity. Pregnancy places demands on the young growing goat. If she has free-choice alfalfa all year along with her browse or grazing, she'll be better equipped for the nutritional demands of pregnancy than if she just grazed on pastures. Young goats who have had enough milk for the first 12 weeks of life are going to be *growthy*, a term used to describe well-nourished kids who have grown big and strong compared to their smaller companions.

Some people use weight to determine when a goat is ready to breed, variously using 75 to 85 pounds as the point of readiness for full-size goats.

Other people use age, breeding does at 7 to 10 months, again depending on date of birth and when they want the babies to arrive.

Still others hold over young goats until the second breeding season. If nutrition is minimal, the kid was born late, or they just don't want more babies the following spring, it may be a good strategy.

KIDDING AROUND

Holding over young goats is costly in several ways. A 2-year-old goat has had two winters of feed invested in her and has no production to contribute for that extra full year. And if you're breeding for improved traits, you miss the earliest chance to evaluate your breeding program.

The female goat's heat, or estrus cycle, is surprisingly similar across all goat breeds. The cycle is usually about 21 days long but can be from 16 to 23 days and still be normal. It's the peak of fertility, with a one- to three-day period where she is actually receptive to the buck and able to conceive a pregnancy. After the period of receptivity, if she's not bred, she will have another cycle ending in another period of receptivity, called "in heat."

How do you know when she's receptive? If an adult buck is in the neighborhood, both he and she will make it pretty clear. The doe will get as close to him as she can—sticking close to common fences or walls. He will be making his buck noises. Chances are neither of them will be very interested in food or anything else besides each other. The doe may become very vocal, too, crying and hollering on the days she's in heat. Her tail will probably wag incessantly. She may have a clear, vaginal mucus discharge. She may become aggressive. She may mount other females in her pen. Or she may do all or none of these behaviors. Each doe is individual in her behaviors, and she may change behavior with each heat cycle as the season progresses. It's called a "silent heat" if she shows no signs of heat. This doe needs to be penned with a buck to ensure she gets bred.

If you don't have a buck at your farm, it's sometimes very difficult to determine when a doe is in heat. The presence of the buck always makes her far more demonstrative. If you need to take your doe to a neighboring buck, watch her carefully and track her heat cycles on a calendar if you can. That way you will eventually be able to predict when her next cycle will be and get her to the buck in plenty of time.

One trick goat owners sometimes use is to get a buck rag—basically an old towel or T-shirt that's been rubbed thoroughly over a buck's scent glands. Keep it in a covered jar or some other airtight container until you suspect your doe is in heat. Then tie it to the fence and watch to see if she shows interest. If she's in heat, and the rag is stinky enough, she will probably show some interest.

When Your Goats Get Pregnant

If your goat doesn't come into heat within about 21 days after breeding, you can safely assume she's pregnant. Pregnancy lasts about 150 days. It varies a few days more or less for different breeds, but five months is standard and a good way to figure due dates. If you want to determine the exact due date, you can go to Fias Co Farm's website, fiascofarm.com/goats/duedate.htm, and use its pregnancy calculator. As long as you know the breeding date, you can calculate the due date.

Don't be alarmed if your goat's pregnancy goes over her due date or if she has her kids before her due date. Just as with people, nature sometimes has its own agenda.

Kids born up to 10 days early usually do fine, although they're skinny, have much shorter hair, and tend to be weaker and often funny-looking for a while. If the babies are more than 10 days premature, they're less likely to survive as in all prematurity.

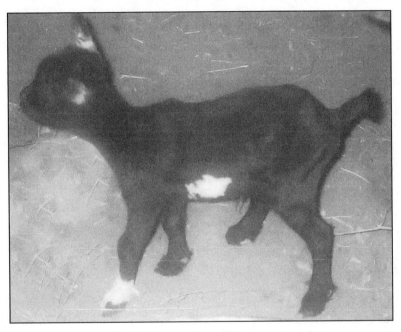

At 10 days premature, this kid is very thin and has prominent bones, an unnatural stance, and unusual proportions.

It's not unheard of for a goat to abort a pregnancy in the first few weeks, but it's usually a result of trauma such as getting butted by a herdmate. An aborted pregnancy might be invisible, but it's often accompanied by a slight bloody discharge. You can try rebreeding her after six weeks or so.

This is the same kid at 2 weeks. She has filled out and grown into more normal proportions.

Caring for the Pregnant Doe

The pregnant doe doesn't need any special food for the first three months of her pregnancy. If you're milking her, continue to milk as normal during this time. Her milk production will gradually decrease on its own. By the time she hits the three-month mark, stop milking her so her body can prepare for the heavy demands of the last 60 days of pregnancy.

If your goat is still giving a large quantity of milk at two and a half or three months before kidding, start skipping one milking a day to help her production decrease. Some very high-producing does will be persistent in production. Skipping a milking each day will be uncomfortable for her for several days, but it's the pressure of a tight udder that triggers her body to decrease the amount of milk she produces. Most goats will be nearly dry at this point without special considerations.

At about the three-month point in her pregnancy, you can begin giving the goat a little grain for extra calories. If you've been milking her until this point, decrease the amount of grain now at milking time, and over the next two months, gradually increase it back to nearly the level you had for a milking doe. For a full-size dairy goat, that's roughly 1½ to 2 pounds twice a day. Use caution, because you don't want your pregnant doe to become too fat, which can cause kidding problems.

GOAT HORN

Research indicates that too much grain during pregnancy is correlated with a higher incidence of kidding problems and low kid survival rates. So don't overdo it!

If your goats are eating grass hay during pregnancy (low in calcium compared to phosphorus) and you feed grain (also low in calcium compared to phosphorus) there's a danger of a low-calcium condition called *hypocalcemia*. (This is discussed in much more detail later in this chapter.) Be sure your mineral mix includes plenty of calcium and is palatable. If at all possible, feed late-stage pregnant does at least a little alfalfa for its higher calcium content.

Some goat breeds have large litters. Some families within breeds tend to have more multiples. Litters of six occur now and then, and five is a fairly common litter size, especially in Nigerian Dwarfs, Kinders, and Nubians. These breeds often have quadruplets but more rarely five or six kids.

As their pregnancy progresses, especially if they're carrying a large number of babies, the more sedentary the goats are likely to get. Goats, like people, need exercise, even when they don't particularly feel like it. Exercise helps position the kids correctly for birth and helps keep the doe from putting on extra fat—both of which pays big dividends at kidding time. You can help by putting their water farther away from their food and shelter. Just the short exercise of walking to the water will be good for does and their future kids.

Observation is always a good care strategy for the pregnant goat. Many health problems have been averted by owners catching something that seems "off" before it gets to be a serious problem.

Signs of Impending Birth

How will you know the babies are coming? Most does give you warning, if you know what to look for.

When the due date is close, start looking for changes in her behavior. The last day of pregnancy is often accompanied by the goat acting quite differently. She may stay off by herself. She may start pawing the ground or bedding. She may quit eating. She may start "talking" to her babies using a soft nicker sound that's unlike her regular noise.

Watch her udder, too. It's been filling up as the pregnancy has advanced, but the last day or two before birth, it really fills up tight and looks shiny. Unfortunately, that's something that can also go on for a few days, so it's not necessarily a for-sure sign the birth is close.

This goat is about to deliver quintuplets.
(Pat Showalter)

The goat has strong ligaments that hold all her pelvic bones together tightly. Those ligaments loosen for birth and their loosening is an indication that birth will occur within about 12 hours. Picture the backbone in the rump area. The ligaments hold the hips to the spine. Before birth, when you touch this area, it feels firm. When those ligaments are loosening, the area feels mushy. The appearance changes also. It looks as though the tailbone has risen up with hollows on either side of it. When you've seen this phenomenon, it's a good indication birth is going to happen soon. Among goat owners, this is called "the ligaments are gone." Of course they're not gone, just far more stretched out and less prominent. Try to observe goats at someone else's farm before you have occasion to try at your own.

One more thing that tells you birth might be happening soon is that she begins to have a mucus discharge. This is commonly referred to as "losing her plug." The mucus can be cloudy at first, but it gradually gets clear, thick, and profuse as the kids start to come out. The mucus sign means birth is very close, no more than hours, and probably less.

HERD HINT

Any of these signs can be either extreme or absent in individual goats. Old-time goat farmers learn to look for clusters of signs. Once you've been through a few births, you'll know your goats' typical behavior.

Pretty soon the goat starts lying down, or getting up and down. You may notice her pushing. This means she's in hard labor. Some goats get noisy; some do not. Normal labor does not last a long time. The length is variable, but an hour of pushing without a baby usually indicates problems. Much longer than an hour means definite trouble.

Remember, the exercise you provided for her and the excellent nutrition all should prevent problems. But you should know when to intervene.

It's Time!

The miracle of birth never ceases to amaze! One day you have one goat, and the next day you have two or more—sometimes many more. It's extraordinary!

Birth is the single event most goat owners cite as their favorite part of raising goats, but it's understandable that not everyone will want to attend the birth. There are fluids that some find offensive. You will have to make your own choice here, but attending births can be life-saving sometimes, for both babies and Mom.

Let's go over what you can expect if you do decide to be at the birth.

As the doe begins pushing, usually you'll see a bubble appear. This is the amniotic membrane enclosing the kid that's in the birth canal. It usually breaks shortly after it appears and is full of a thick, slippery fluid that makes the kid's birth easier.

This goat has just started hard labor and is pushing.
(Pat Showalter)

The first kid of a litter should be born toes and nose first—they "dive" into the world. The hardest job for the doe is pushing out the head. Once that happens, the rest of the body slips out with very little effort. It's important at this point that the kid can breathe. If her nose is covered with fluid or the membrane, clean it off. If you're going to bottle-raise the kids, don't wait for the mother to do the cleaning. Have a selection of old towels nearby and be sure to clean the face very well. Mothers very often are busy at this point starting on the next kid.

The normal position for the second kid can be back feet first. At this point, the birth canal has been stretched by the first kid so there's little chance of the head getting stuck. If the first kid comes out back feet first, the head sometimes hangs up, possibly causing the kid to inhale amniotic fluid, which is deadly. The third and subsequent kids can come out any direction at all.

She's just starting to push out her first baby.
(Pat Showalter)

She has delivered the first and is delivering the second kid.
(Pat Showalter)

It's only with the first kid that the position is important. What happens when the position isn't correct? Most of the time—especially if you've provided good care—nature takes its course and babies are born without problems. Cleaning off the nose so they can breathe well is something I recommend, but that's about all you should have to do if everything goes well.

But if there are problems, the amount of "helping" you do could be much more. It might be as simple as pulling gently on the kids' feet when Mom is pushing to help get them out. That can be important if the kid is big and Mom is small. Helping is safe if you're clean and gentle. Remember that legs are slippery, so wrap a part of a towel around them and pull only when the doe is pushing. Whatever the slope of her rump, pull parallel to that slope. So if she's standing, pull slightly downward, not straight out behind. She's usually not standing up, but the angle relative to her structure is the same regardless of her position. If the kid is large, sometimes pulling a bit harder on just one leg helps the shoulders come more easily.

If the doe has been pushing for a while with no progress, it could indicate the babies are tangled or they're in a position that's not favorable for birth (*dystochia*). Positions in this category are nose but no feet or only one foot, tail but no back feet, front feet but no head, and worst of all, backbone presenting.

DEFINITION

Dystochia is a birth presentation that's unlikely to result in an unassisted birth.

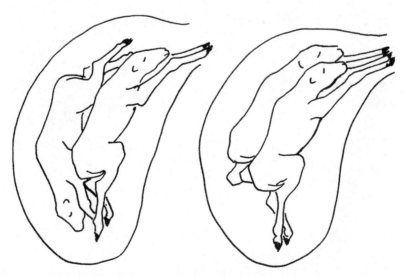

Two birth positions. One (left) is a perfect presentation for twins, but the other (right) shows a traffic-jam positioning.
(Veralyn Srch-Harelson)

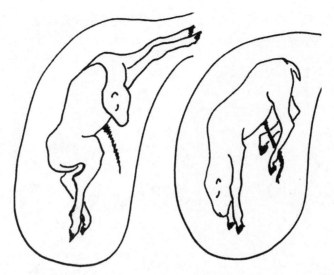

These two problem birth positions will require assistance for the kids to be born.
(Veralyn Srch-Harelson)

Either you, your mentor, or your veterinarian must address dystochia. If the babies won't come out on their own, both mother and babies will die. Assistance involves putting a very clean hand or a gloved hand inside the doe to find the right body parts to enable the kids to be born.

This isn't the place for a complete treatise on that process, but some positions are fairly easy to sort out. Others are very difficult. When just the nose is showing, it's fairly simple to find and present the feet, but if the neck is bent around toward the kid's body, it's very difficult, sometimes requiring a c-section. Fishing out babies is difficult because there's not much room to work, and you can tear the uterus, which is fatal for the doe, if you're not knowledgeable and very careful.

GOAT HORN

Birthing problems aren't the norm, but you should consider how you'll handle them should they arise. Do you have mentors with the know-how to help? Do you have a veterinarian you can call on? The time to find help or a veterinarian is not when you need them, but far ahead of that time.

Assuming the kids are born normally and all goes well, the normal presentation also breaks or tears the umbilical cord as the kid arrives. There may be a little blood, but the tearing tends to stop the bleeding. Cutting the cord would cause more bleeding and is almost never necessary. If it hasn't torn on its own within a few minutes of birth, tie it off with dental floss and then cut it.

Once the doe has delivered her kids, she will begin expelling the afterbirth. This can take a few minutes or up to several hours. Do not tug on it. If it persists 12 hours or more, talk to your veterinarian. Goats will have a slight bloody discharge for up to two weeks after birth. This is normal.

The first kids are getting up and Mom is beginning to deliver the afterbirth.
These fluid-filled sacks are normal after delivery.
(Pat Showalter)

Caring for Your Newborns

If your baby goats are born in a relatively clean area, that's a good thing. A clean birthing area is always preferable. Remember that on their bellies, they have the open end of the umbilical cord through which bacteria could enter. If that happens and an infection starts, it is called *navel ill*. The symptoms appear in a kid usually less than a week old running a temperature and refusing to eat because the infection at her navel hurts when warm milk sits near it. If untreated, it spreads to joints. Treatment is penicillin by injection for five to seven days. As insurance, many people dip the navel cord into a strong iodine solution. It certainly can't hurt, and it might even help.

Feeding Newborns

Newborns receive some passive immunity from their dams during pregnancy; this lasts about six weeks. They receive more immunity from the colostrum produced by their dams. Whether you choose to dam-raise or bottle-raise, the kids need to drink that colostrum within the first few hours of life. Either milk the mother immediately and feed the kids the colostrum, or be sure the kids are up and nursing on their dam.

Be prepared to bottle-feed kids, even if you want them to be raised by their dams. Sometimes a doe dies, leaving orphans. Sometimes Mom rejects a newborn and won't allow her to nurse. It's possible to restrain the doe and allow the kids to nurse while she cannot move away or try to hurt them. It is time-consuming (at least four times a day at first, and more often would be better), but it might make her a more agreeable mother. It also might not. Always be prepared to bottle-feed.

HERD HINT

If your kids will nurse from the dam, help them get started by squeezing the teats to be sure a stream of colostrum comes out. That cleans out any plugged material and ensures the kids are getting nourishment.

How much milk should bottle-raised kids get? That's a common question. The newborn should get as much milk as she wants at least four times a day for the first few days. Depending on your time commitments, you could go to three feedings a day within the first week or 10 days. Remember that the amount of milk they get determines how big and how fast they grow.

Give full-size dairy goats all they want until their total consumption is about 2 quarts of milk a day or just slightly less. For miniatures, that amount is about 1 quart per day. More than that doesn't give you better results. Less than that means they'll grow slower and not reach maximum stature for early breeding. For people who want to breed the females to kid at about 13 to 15 months, optimum growth is important.

At about a month old, the kids can go to twice-a-day feedings, with the total still staying around 2 quarts.

Some people wean the young at 8 to 10 weeks. Weaning at 12 weeks is more likely to get optimal results, but it's not always feasible. The kids develop much better if not weaned from milk until they're chewing their cuds well, which can be from 8 to 13 weeks. Whatever you decide, the last couple weeks of bottle-feeding is the time to start decreasing the amount of milk in their bottles so that by weaning time, the last bottle is only about 12 ounces and they're off to solid feed only.

All changes in type and in amount of feed (but especially milk) should be gradual.

Vaccinations for Kids

At 4 to 6 weeks, the kids need a vaccination for Clostridium (overeating disease) and tetanus. Check with your mentor, your veterinarian, and your suppliers. In some areas, other vaccinations or combinations are appropriate where different diseases are prevalent. The Cd&T (Clostridium and Tetanus) vaccination requires a booster in three to four weeks. There's some variation in the time for vaccinations depending on whom you talk to, so check with your veterinarian.

Not all goat owners choose to vaccinate their animals. If you castrate or disbud your goats, at the very least, a tetanus vaccination is *very* good insurance.

Goat Growth and Development

From newborn to fully grown adult goat takes about two years. The newborn, while she may be up on her feet within minutes or hours after birth, is likely to be wobbly for a day or so and will sleep a lot. By a few days old, she will be running and bouncing. By the time she's a month old or less, she can run up to a wall and jump halfway up, hitting all four feet and bouncing back to the ground. Little goats are enormous fun to watch!

Many factors affect the growth of goats. Nutrition is the biggest one. Goats who get less-than-optimal nutrition can be stunted. Sometimes, with better nutrition later on, they will eventually catch up, but not always. Genetics also plays a role in growth and development, but it's difficult to separate the effects unless the nutrition requirements are already met. The old adage "You can't starve a profit out of goats," makes oodles of sense. Feed as well as you can possibly manage.

Another thing that affects growth and development are *coccidia* and other parasites. Coccidia are much more serious for very young goats—they seem to pick them up almost immediately. The coccidia life cycle is 21 days, and by time a goat is 21 days old, a big coccidia load could be having a serious effect on the goat's growth. I cover coccidia more in the next chapter, but for now, be aware that coccidia are ubiquitous and are passed through fecal matter, so preventing infection is all about keeping fecal matter out of places where baby goats can be infected. Serious diarrhea around 3 weeks of age is typical of a problematic coccidia infection.

Kid goats' feet grow just as adult goats' do. It's even more important to be sure the kids' feet are trimmed correctly while they're growing so rapidly. Check them at 4 weeks to see how much growth there is, and plan your trimming schedule accordingly.

The condition of the young goat is more important than what she weighs, although the two will be correlated. Good condition means a shiny coat, enough flesh to cover the bones, and lots of energy. If the goat's thin, then she's not getting enough to eat or she has a parasite problem. Some Nigerians will start life at less than 2 pounds and be only 40 pounds at breeding, while some Nubians can start life at over 12 pounds and weigh almost 100 pounds at breeding. An overly fat goat is no healthier than an underweight one. Look at her ribs. You should be able to barely see the outline of them under the skin. If the skin sinks down between the ribs, she's too thin.

DEFINITION

Coccidia are one-celled microorganisms that damage the cells of the goat's digestive tract. A big coccidia load can cause bloody diarrhea in severe infestations. **Precocious udder** is an early development of half or all of the udder on a very young doe kid.

Some female kids will have some udder development, or *precocious udder*, before puberty. While not common, it's not terribly abnormal either, but you don't need to treat it in any way. Puberty comes anywhere from 2 to 6 months. To test for sexual maturity, gently roll one of her teats between your fingers. If you can feel the teat canal within the teat, she's at sexual maturity. Breeding is still best done by weight, though.

The time and the food you invest in a young goat can have huge dividends for your goat's productivity down the line. Feed your goats well, address their needs, and you'll have more to show for it.

There's no doubt about it: kids have a high cuteness factor.

The Least You Need to Know

- Male goats have some behaviors that are on the obnoxious and smelly side.
- Breeding season is from August to January for many breeds, and heat cycles are usually 21 days long.
- Pregnancy lasts about 150 days, and the pregnant goat needs little extra care until about the last 60 days of pregnancy.
- If you want to watch the births, it helps to know the signs of impending birth, what the birth should look like, and when you should intervene.
- Caring for baby goats requires decisions about bottle feeding as well as other factors.
- Happy, healthy kids will grow and develop in somewhat standard ways. Knowing what out-of-the-ordinary things to look for helps head off problems later on.

Protecting Your Goats

In This Chapter

- Keeping your goats safe from predators
- Keeping your goats safe from parasites
- Vaccinations for your goats
- Tips for giving shots

Goats are far from the top of the food chain. There are many predators above them and a few below who consider goats a delicacy. You must become their protector from all those predators. If you don't have enough information or the tools to protect your goats, it can cost you heartache, time, and money.

Most goats are more like pets to their owners than livestock. It's always sad when you lose a pet, but even worse if you see them killed by dogs, coyotes, or other wildlife. An attack that leaves them maimed can be even worse. Parasites, though lowly on the food chain, can also destroy and maim. In fact, they could end up costing you plenty in lost production over a long period of time. So let's identify the potentials for harm and loss and do what's possible to minimize or eliminate them.

Protecting Your Goats from Predators

Many kinds of predators love to eat goats, including dogs, coyotes, bears, and mountain lions. Of these, dogs are responsible for more goat losses than all the rest. Of particular danger are domestic neighbor dogs. When allowed to run loose, they often run in packs. They may be wonderfully sweet when they're on their own front porch, but something feral and mean switches on in their brain when they run with other domestic dogs and they often kill just for sport, not due to lack of food.

Today, many rural farms have been carved from territory once belonging to predatory carnivores like big cats, bears, wolves, and coyotes. When their natural food sources become scarce from drought, shrinking habitat, or other environmental stressors, these animals look for something easy to eat ... like your goats.

Human predators can be a big problem in some areas, too. Those who want a goat barbecue or a milk producer sometimes steal what they want rather than buy it. None of these have to be inevitable losses if you learn how to properly protect your goats. In theory, you could design a predator-proof fence to keep harm from your goats. A fence like that, though, would be very pricey.

Goat Guard Dogs

People raise goats and sheep in almost every region of the world. These herders have developed specialized dogs to protect their herds or flocks. Collectively, these dogs are called *livestock guardian dogs* (*LGDs*). LGDs have evolved in different countries, but all have ended up with similar traits:

- They are big.
- They often are white, although not always.
- They live with the herd and consider the sheep or goats "their" family.
- They are very protective of their herd.
- The dogs are fairly independent of people and do not need direction or commands to protect the goats.

DEFINITION

Livestock guardian dogs (**LGDs**) are herd-protecting dogs who work on their own to keep predators at bay.

LGDs often act as a deterrent to predators more than as attack animals. They do attack when needed, but more often than not you'll see them patrolling the area where their goats live. At the slightest hint of a threat, they bark and face the danger, which is usually enough to prevent most predator attacks. When it's not, LGDs are valiant in attacking intruders. The livestock world is full of amazing stories of LGDs fighting, even to the death, to protect their herd. In areas with many or big predators, LGDs stand a better chance of success when they work in pairs.

A livestock guardian dog watches over her charge.

Because of their independence, LGDs are more successful when they are *not* treated like the family dog. They do need to understand who their human family is, but they should be socialized primarily with the goats. A good LGD knows the difference between his family and strangers and will treat strangers like a threat until given the okay or introduction by his humans. If you're in an area where humans are a problem, that's a very good characteristic.

KIDDING AROUND

I once had septic tank problems at my farm and called a service company to come out and diagnose the problem. The workman showed up, and I headed off to the area where the septic tank was buried, with him following me. I was several yards ahead of the man when my LGD appeared and put herself between the man and me. She didn't bark or growl, but she planted herself in a decidedly aggressive and protective stance as if to say, "Stop! You better not come any closer!" As soon as I realized what was going on, I went back and introduced her to the man, and she was fine with him from then on.

There are many breeds of LGDs because they come from many cultures. The first LGD to be imported into this country was the Great Pyrenees from the Pyrenees Mountains between France and Spain. As the LGD phenomenon has gained momentum in this country, more breeds have been imported. They include these, among others:

- The Akbash and Anatolian from Turkey
- The Komondor and Kuvasz from Hungary
- The Maremma from Italy
- The Caucasian Ovtcharka from Russia
- The Tibetan Mastiff and Kyi-Apso from Tibet
- The Sharplaninac from Yugoslavia
- The Estrela Mountain Dog of Portugal
- The Tatra from Poland
- The Karakachan from Bulgaria

Some of these are now common in the United States, some are only found in their countries of origin, and some are becoming rare even in their native lands.

The different breeds are quite similar in lots of ways, but there are minor differences, primarily in size of territory and aggressiveness. Most common in U.S. goat herds today are the Pyrenees and the Anatolian. I've had both, and I prefer a cross-breed of the two. It seems to have the best characteristics of both parent breeds, being less aggressive than the Anatolian, less inclined to wander than the Pyrenees, and with shorter hair like its Turkish side. However, if you talk with anyone who owns an LGD, you'll find strong preferences for several breeds and all with good reasons.

Some breeds of LGD tend to "expand" their territory. They may try to get out of their own pasture to include neighboring farms under their charge. It is imperative that you have excellent fencing if you use an LGD.

Nearly all livestock guardian dogs have strong instincts for guarding the animals they're raised with. But as puppies, they also have a tendency to play with the goats. Some breeds tend to play harder, and with more potential damage, than others. They need strong supervision to learn that playing with the goats is not okay. Pyrenees usually do a decent job of guarding by the time they're 6 to 8 months old, although they're not big enough or mature enough then to go head to head with a predator. Anatolians tend to take longer to reach maturity and responsibility—closer to 18 months. Cross-breeds seem to mature earlier and will often be working well before they're a year old.

KIDDING AROUND

When my LGD Zoey was about 4 months old, she lived in a small pen with Nigerian Dwarf goats. I could watch her from the house, and when I saw her playing with the goats, I'd scold her from a window—immediate feedback for bad behavior. It was very effective, and her behavior got better and better. One day, however, I heard a terrible screaming noise from the goat pen. It was the distinctive noise made only by a new baby goat in a life-threatening situation. I ran to the pen and rushed inside only to find Zoey carefully carrying a newborn Nigerian around in her mouth. There wasn't a scratch on the goat, but the baby sure thought she was a goner. The dog was scolded, and she never pulled that one again.

Talk to anyone who has an LGD or two, and they'll tell you the dog is worth his weight in gold for peace of mind and freedom from worry about predators.

Other Goat Guarders

Some goat owners swear by guard llamas and guard donkeys. These animals can be very protective, and use their feet and body weight to fight off predators such as dogs.

There are some drawbacks, however. Donkeys and llamas can also be prey for the big predators, so they're unlikely to provide any deterrent for big cats or bears. I once heard a story about a guard llama attacking a woman who was in the pen with the owner. Intact jack donkeys often attack their charges when they become sexually mature. Female donkeys may attack any strange human they think threatens their herd. This information makes me skeptical of their overall usefulness, although I have no personal experience. Nevertheless, if either of these appeals to you, talk to people who use them.

Protecting Your Goats from Parasites

Parasites live on or inside your goats. They are ubiquitous and part of any livestock operation. Some parasites are unique to goats, and some are found in many species. Parasites hurt your goats, and they hurt your pocketbook.

Parasites don't make a living on their own. They are freeloaders on your goats and, ultimately, on you. They survive by taking something from your goat. Most take some of her blood or live in her tissues, where they do damage. Your goat is therefore giving away her resources that could be going into making milk, babies, meat, or fiber. You're providing those resources. They're not going into what you want, and they cost you money and production.

Parasites also make your goat more likely to get sick and cost you for veterinarian visits and medicines. And the greatest loss of all: parasites can kill. That's not only a financial loss but probably an emotional one, too.

Let's look at the four main groupings of these little beasts and ways to deal with them.

Coccidia (Protozoa)

Coccidia, mentioned briefly in Chapter 6, are in the group Protozoa, single-celled organisms that are particularly hard on young goats. At some point in their life cycle, coccidia make their way into the cells lining the digestive tract. The normal job of those cells is to absorb nutrients from the digestive tract. The coccidia in these cells multiply, undergo changes, and multiply some more. On the twenty-first day of their life cycle, they burst out of the cell, completely destroying it. A 3-week-old goat with a heavy infestation of coccidia can have a sudden and severe case of *bloody scours*. Loss of all those cells also has an impact on the goat's ability to absorb adequate nutrients. It becomes a downward spiral as the escaped organisms reproduce and start the cycle all over.

DEFINITION

Bloody scours is a term used to denote diarrhea with blood in it often caused by coccidia or other parasites.

If you can keep the coccidia in check in young goats, they do develop some immunity to them over time. Coccidia are not usually a big problem for adults. The danger is that severe infections can do enough damage—some of it permanent—to stunt growth or create an adult who will never be able to absorb enough nutrients to maintain body condition. An adult doe who tends to get thinner and thinner as her lactation progresses (in spite of available good nutrition) may have some permanent damage to her digestive tract from an early coccidia overload.

Cestodes

The Cestodes group includes tapeworms. About half the tapeworms goats pick up, from dogs and pastures, are not dangerous. But a tapeworm sheds body segments in the feces that look a little like grains of rice in their goat berries. They're very noticeable. When tapeworms cause problems in goats, it's often in young animals, who then have poor growth and sometimes a pot-bellied appearance as a result.

There are two things to remember about tapeworms even if they don't usually cause disease:

- They are eating some of the feed you are paying for, feed that's not nourishing your goat.

- When goats have tapeworms, it's an indication that they may have heavy infestations of other parasites. Tapeworms can be an indicator of more serious parasite problems.

Trematodes

Trematodes include liver flukes. Flukes need snails as an intermediate host in their life cycle, so they are common in wet areas. When the goat eats the grass blade with a snail on it, they become infected.

Flukes live in the goat's liver, causing damage. Severe infestations can cause death.

Nematodes

Warm, wet conditions that favor flukes and coccidia are the same conditions that favor other parasites, especially the group Nematodes, or roundworms. There are lots of roundworms, but the worst of them all is *Haemonchus contortus*, also called the bankrupt worm, barber-pole worm, or stomach worm. This bad guy is a gluttonous blood-sucker.

Goats with a severe infestation of *Haemonchus* or other roundworms can become very anemic and die from it. It's difficult—although not impossible—to control this parasite because it has the most resistance to worming medicines. The other parasite groups pale in comparison to the damage caused by this one.

Goats who are thin, are listless, have rough hair, and generally look bad are probably dealing with an overload of parasites, and *Haemonchus contortus* is usually the main problem.

Keeping Parasites Under Control

Controlling parasites starts with sanitation and feeding practices. All parasites that live inside your goat produce eggs to complete their life cycle. Those eggs are passed out of the goat in fecal matter. Keeping feet that have fecal matter on them out of food and water helps control the parasites.

If goats graze on pastures, the eggs in their fecal matter hatch in warm, wet weather, and the larval stages crawl up the blades of grass, where the goats then eat them. If your goats must graze on grass, rotate the pastures, and use wormers effectively on the goats before they go on to clean pastures so they're less likely to spread more parasite eggs. Also, do not overgraze pastures. Fewer blades of grass just mean more parasite larvae on each blade of grass. Browsers will have less trouble with parasites because the food is too high off the ground for larval infestation.

KIDDING AROUND

Parasites cannot survive long in heat or dry conditions. If you live where there is a very severe winter, most environmental parasites will be killed over the winter. It's the milder, wetter climates and especially warm, wet climates that have the most difficulty with parasites.

Identifying Parasites

So how do you know what parasites you might have in your goats and how to deal with them? Not all parasites are treated the same, which is why it's important to know what's bugging your goats.

The definitive test is called a fecal exam or flotation exam, and it's done by any competent laboratory and most veterinarians' offices. A few goat berries are smashed, added to a solution, and the microscopic eggs that rise to the surface are counted. (In this description, I have condensed the process considerably.) The lab can tell you if your egg counts are high, medium, or low and what kind of critter they came from. The fee for the test varies widely. University agricultural labs will probably have the lowest cost and the best accuracy, but if that's not available to you, ask your veterinarian.

It's not necessary to do a fecal test on all your goats. If they're in the same pen and roughly the same age, they probably all have the same parasites. So testing can involve combining a few goat berries from two goats in a pen for an alternative testing method.

The meat goat industry has developed a color chart you can compare to the mucous membranes around the goat's eye. If they're nice and pink, she isn't anemic. As the membranes get lighter and lighter, you know your goat is more severely infected with parasites, usually *Haemonchus*. This test, FAMACHA, is not definitive because it doesn't tell you what's lurking, only that some are. Using this test probably makes sense for large herds, but it does leave a lot to be desired. It's going to be better for production if the membrane pinkness never fades on your goats. Any anemia has an impact on production.

Treating Parasites

Now let's look at the medicines that treat for parasites and how to use them. The medicines are called worming medicines or, more correctly, *anthelmintics*.

DEFINITION

Anthelmintics, or *antihelminthics,* are drugs that expel parasitic worms from the body by either stunning or killing them.

In the eyes of animal medicine manufacturers, goats are a minor species and don't get the same attention as sheep and cows. Most of the medicines are designed for those, so the *dosage and instructions* are for cows or sheep. Goats have a much faster metabolism than cows, which means they need medicines either in higher doses or more often. Treating goats with cow medicines is called "off label" and must be done under the supervision of a veterinarian. (Be sure your veterinarian is knowledgeable about goats! Not all are.) You need to learn as much as you can, too.

Let's go back to the first parasite, coccidia. The treatment for coccidia is a group of sulfa drugs. They are sulfamethiazine, sulfadimethoxine (Albon), and sulfaquanidine, usually given for five days. You can purchase Albon (12.5 percent solution) from supply houses (like Jeffers, see Appendix B). Sulmet and DiMethox as well as Albon are dosed orally at the following schedule:

> *Day 1:* 1 cubic centimeter (cc) per 5 pounds body weight
>
> *Days 2 through 5:* 1 cc per 10 pounds body weight

Sulfas do *not* taste good, and even small goats will probably fight taking it. Nevertheless, it is the most effective treatment for coccidia. It could be added to bottles or other taste-camouflaging foods. There is a banana-flavored Albon goats love, but it's more costly and takes more volume.

There are products you can buy called coccidiostats that you feed the goats every day to prevent coccidia from getting a foothold. The brand names are Bovatec, Rumensin, and Decox.

> **GOAT HORN**
>
> Coccidiostats are toxic to horses. Do not use them if you have horses!

Worming medicine for tapeworms are praziquantel, epsiprantel, fenbendazole (Safeguard), and mebendazole. There may be others your veterinarian recommends.

For the flukes, the two medicines used are Curatrem or Ivomec Plus. Both contain a drug specifically for flukes. Ask your vet for dosage information.

Now we get to the Nematodes, *Haemonchus*, and other roundworms. They are more dangerous, more difficult to eliminate, and present more resistance to the drugs. It's pretty well accepted that the "white" (the benzimidazoles) and "clear" (the levamisoles) wormers aren't effective for these parasites. Most goat owners use the macrolides (Ivomec, Dectomax, Eprinex, and Cydectin). This is a subject fraught with controversy, so you'll need help from your veterinarian, your mentors, and other knowledgeable goat people to decide which is appropriate for your goats.

A Few Additional Notes on Wormers

Most wormers are dosed according to the animal's weight. If the cow dose is 1 cc per 100 pounds, it would translate to less than 2 ccs for most full-size adult goats. Two things come into play here. Due to goat metabolism, 1 cc per 100 pounds is low. And guessing the weight of your goat is hard to do—even experienced goat people usually guess low.

It's possible that the combination of underestimating weight and using cattle dosage has contributed to resistance. Dr. Craig Downie of Bailey Veterinary Clinic in Roseburg, Oregon, one of the most knowledgeable goat vets I ever met, told me Ivomec is safe up to 20 times the cow dose, even for pregnant goats. This is for Ivomec only, not Cydectin. The often-recommended dose for Cydectin is 1 cc per 20 pounds, but talk to your vet.

In some parts of the country, it is recommended that deworming products always be given orally, regardless of how they're labeled. The only exception is when treating for meningeal worms, which requires injecting the animal with Ivomec. This protocol is now in disfavor, and they're back to recommending injectables.

Once you find a product that works for your herd, continue using it for at least a year before switching to another product. Switching will speed up the likelihood of resistance. If a product no longer works well in your herd, you can still use it in combination with another deworming product from a different class (Ivomec and

Safeguard, for example, or Eprinex and Valbazen). Use both products full strength at the same time to achieve the best results.

Animals should be dewormed at least once during the winter, and most people worm immediately after kidding. The worming frequency depends on your climate, your management practices, and the results of good testing.

Ivermectin (Ivomec, Double Impact, Zimecterin, Equimectrin, Rotectin 1) comes in injectable or paste form. Most injectables contain 1 percent ivermectin, while the equine paste formulations contain 2 percent. Oral dose for the injectable equine products is 1 cc per 50 pounds. Put the dosage ring on the weight that's twice what your goat weighs. (For example, for a 125-pound goat, put the weight ring on 250 pounds.) Underdosing is more hazardous than overdosing.

KIDDING AROUND

Ivomec attacks the parasite's nerve tissue. Nematodes and other roundworms have "naked" nerves with no myelin sheath. Mammals have a myelin sheath protecting their nerves. That's why it doesn't hurt your goats but still kills the roundworms. Ivomec and Strongid are also used to treat people in third-world countries where human parasites are rampant.

Doramectin (Dectomax) is an injectable cattle dewormer in the same class as products like ivermectin. If parasites are resistant to ivermectin dewormers, they will probably be resistant to doramectin and eprinomectin products, too. Oral dose is 1 cc per 50 pounds.

Eprinomectin (Eprinex) is a pour-on cattle dewormer in the ivermectin class. Give to goats orally at the rate of 5 ccs per 110 pounds. That's the same as the pour-on rate for cattle.

Moxidectin (Cydectin or Quest) is also an option. Either Cydectin pour-on cattle dewormer or Quest horse gel dewormer can be used in goats to control most parasites, except tapeworms. Quest contains a higher percentage of moxidectin than Cydectin. Recommended dosage for Cydectin is 5 ccs per 110 pounds. For Quest, put the dose ring on the weight that is closest to your animal's weight.

Albendazole (Valbazen) is a white liquid oral dewormer that should not be given to pregnant does in the first month of pregnancy. It causes birth defects if given too early in pregnancy. The recommended dosage for goats is 8 ccs per 100 pounds and is most effective for tapeworms, or used in conjunction with another class of dewormer.

Fenbendazole (Safeguard or Panacur), either liquid or paste, like Valbazen, is most effective when used for tapeworms or in conjunction with another class of dewormer. Recommended dosage for goats is at least twice the cattle dosage (approximately 5 ccs per 100 pounds if the product is 10 percent).

Oxfendazole (Synanthic) is another white liquid product. The recommended dosage is 5 ccs per 110 pounds of body weight.

Levamisole (Levasole, Tramisol, Prohibit) is an older deworming product that is gaining renewed use as parasites are building up resistance to some of the newer products. Take extreme care not to overdose because it can be fatal. Use at the recommended sheep dosage.

All this information on worming medicines indicates that the problems with resistance may sometimes be caused by inadequate information, resulting in poor dosing. Maybe it's not so much about resistance as we usually think of it. But check with your medical adviser.

Here's one more bit of information to help you protect your goats: all wormers kill or eliminate only the adult worms. Remember the fecal test that told you what worms and how many were in your goat? It did that by counting worm eggs. The medication didn't kill those eggs, and they don't just go away. Even if your worming medicine kills every adult, all those eggs still inside your goat hatch! And there's your goat, full of parasites again.

The solution—and it amazes me that it's rarely recommended—is to use the same correct dose of worming medicine again in 10 days, and again at 21 days. The worm life cycle is 21 days, so the subsequent treatments should get all the eggs that hatch after the first worming. Retest at four weeks to see how effective your regimen was.

Not everyone chooses to use the wormers I've mentioned here. Some people swear by herbal wormers, but unless you're testing, it's only a guess if they really work. And of course, it's good management to use practices that minimize exposure to parasites. Good mineral supplementation dramatically increases parasite resistance, too. Studies show that lambs (similar to goats) have 95 percent fewer roundworms when their copper reserves are medium-high. Be sure your goats are not copper-deficient.

Vaccinations

The most common vaccination in goats is the Cd&T (Clostridium and Tetanus) vaccine mentioned in Chapter 6. It vaccinates against Clostridium Perfringens types C and D and also against tetanus. Goats are at the greatest risk for tetanus during disbudding and castrating. Still, some people choose not to vaccinate and often have no problems. Clostridium causes overeating disease that can strike the biggest and best of the young, especially when they've overeaten but sometimes for no apparent reason.

The dosage is 2 ccs per goat, no matter her size. Kids get their first vaccination at 4 to 6 weeks, with a booster four weeks later and again four weeks after that. Some people give boosters to both kids and adults twice a year, and some only once.

Both tetanus and Clostridium are killers and heartbreaking to experience. This vaccination is easy, inexpensive, and good insurance against both—although with goats, nothing is foolproof!

There are vaccinations for pneumonia used in cattle, rarely in goats, but there is an intranasal vaccine for Bovine Rhinotracheitis, Parainfluenza, called Nasalgen that's sometimes used in goats when they're going to be under unusual stress like going to shows or moving to a new home. It should be used three or four weeks prior to the show or move to provide the best immunity.

Some people use an eight-way clostridial vaccine in areas of red water disease. This is a problem specifically in the Pacific Northwest and gulf coastal states.

Other vaccines have some uses in some situations, but these are the most commonly used in goats.

Giving Your Goats Shots

How do you give your goats all these medicines? Some of the worming medicines are given orally. But there are three ways to give medicines in a shot:

- Intravenous (IV), or in a vein (This should only be done by veterinarians.)
- Intramuscular (IM), or in a muscle
- Subcutaneous (Sub-Q), or under the skin

Most veterinarians now agree that goat muscles aren't big enough to make a difference between IM and Sub-Q. So for our purposes, we're only looking at the Sub-Q shots. They are as effective and have less risk of doing nerve damage or hitting a blood vessel.

Methods and styles of shots vary with the individuals who give them. I've tried many ways and locations on the goat, and the following is my preference. It's simple and effective, and it seems to work for the goats, too.

First, you must prepare the syringe. If it comes with a needle attached, great. If not, you must carefully attach the needle and keep it sterile. The syringe and the needle come with covers. Remove the hub end of the needle cover, put the needle's attachment onto the small end of the syringe, and give it a little twist to tighten. Don't touch the tip of the syringe with your fingers, and don't touch any part of the needle except the covers.

Clean the top of the medicine bottle's rubber top with alcohol. If you need 5 ccs of medicine, remove the needle cover, pull back the plunger to the 5-cc mark, and insert the needle into the bottle. Push the plunger to inject the 5 ccs of air into the bottle and then turn the bottle and syringe upside down and withdraw 5 ccs of medicine. Injecting the air into the bottle first prevents forming a vacuum caused by taking liquid out of an airtight bottle.

HERD HINT

For viscous (thick) medicines, use an 18-gauge needle. For very watery medicines like Cd&T vaccine, use a 20- or 22-gauge needle. Use needles that are ½ to 1 inch long for all applications.

The goat must be restrained. A milking stand works well for this, or just leaning her against a fence with your hip against her neck might work. If your goat isn't too tall and you have long-enough legs, you might try straddling the goat's neck, facing her tail.

The shot should go in the loose skin over her rib cage, at least midway down her side. There are two reasons for this: it's very loose skin, and there are fewer nerve endings there.

You don't need to use alcohol on the goat's skin.

If you're right-handed, hold the syringe in your right hand, lift a tent of skin on her left side with your left hand about an inch from her body, and insert the needle between your fingers holding the tent and her body, pointing downward. Be careful not to go through both layers of skin. Slowly inject the medicine out of the syringe, remove the needle from the goat, recap the needle, and dispose of it properly. Gently rub the area of the shot on the goat to decrease any irritation and disperse the medicine.

This is one of the most effective and easiest ways to give a goat a shot.
(Nathaniel Kemper)

Goats who are well fed, who have good mineral levels (especially copper), and who have few stressors will have a stronger immune system than goats who don't have those advantages. Much of keeping goats healthy involves simply providing what they need for optimal health. If your goats are often ailing in some way, you might need to look at your feeding and management practices to see what improvements could help with overall herd health. The dividends are well worth the effort.

The Least You Need to Know

- Livestock guardian dogs (LGDs) are one of the best ways to protect your goats from predators.
- You can minimize parasite problems with proper management strategies.

- Different parasites cause different problems for your goats. Knowing what's bugging your goats is the first step in treating them.
- A few common vaccinations are used in the goat world.
- To administer medicines and vaccinations, you need to know how to safely and effectively give your goats shots.

What If They Get Sick?

In This Chapter

- Diagnosing health problems by symptoms
- Dealing with problems, from nose to tail
- Diagnosing udder or milk problems
- Understanding neurological problems
- What to do if a goat goes down or even dies

No matter how much prevention you practice with your goats, sometimes things go wrong. I don't want to imply that all the following things will happen, but I do want to emphasize that if anything goes wrong, you need to have a clue about what needs to be done—either by you or by your veterinarian.

When goats are repeatedly having health issues, it's a warning sign that you might need to look more closely at your mineral supplementation or some other area of your management. Are the goats stressed? Does your dog chase them? Are they getting enough to eat? Are they overcrowded? Whenever they're stressed, that's when problems are likely to show up.

Observe and Report

The best way to prevent serious health problems is observation. When you look carefully at your goats each day, you'll notice changes immediately in how they look or behave. Small differences could mean the start of big problems. Catching problems at the start keeps most things small and insignificant. Letting little changes go unnoticed, however, may mean big costs or even losses.

Get in the habit of running your hand down each goat from her head across her backbone to her tail. Every day. Most goats like it, most people like it, and you never know when it might reveal a lump or bump or twitch that shouldn't be there.

If you need to call your veterinarian, be prepared. At the very least, he's going to ask what the goat's temperature is. The temperature tells the vet a lot. Do you know how to take the temp? Use a good thermometer, shaken down and inserted gently, rectally. Leave it in for five minutes. You can use lubricants like KY Jelly or just dishwashing soap like Palmolive if you need to. Next, the vet will ask about the goat's symptoms. Tell him what's different, how she's acting, or what she's doing. He'll also want to know how long the symptoms have been going on. You must have this information in hand before you call, so be sure to do your homework!

> **HERD HINTS**
>
> What's "normal" for goats? In general, a healthy goat's temperature is 102°F to 103°F, although it might be higher if it's hot out. A healthy goat's pulse rate is 70 to 80 beats per minute, and her respiration is 15 to 30 per minute. Rumen (stomach) movements are 1 or 1½ per minute.

Let's look at the categories of symptoms so you can find them quickly in the event you need to know.

Runny Noses, Coughing, and Fevers

A runny nose isn't normal for a goat and is usually indicative of an upper-respiratory infection. To check if it's serious, take the goat's temperature. If the temperature is elevated, the goat probably needs antibiotics. With an elevated temperature, runny nose (or any kind of discharge), and especially when combined with coughing, pneumonia is likely the cause, and the goat needs antibiotics. Consult your veterinarian. Some will make suggestions and allow you to give your own antibiotics. Commonly used medicines for pneumonia are penicillin, penicillin-type medicines (Excenel), and Nuflor, but check with your medical adviser for dosage and frequency. Pneumonia is somewhat contagious, but more often results from stressors in your goat's environment.

GOAT HORN

Most antibiotics and other medicines given to goats have a withdrawal time for both milk and meat. Residues of the medicine remain in the milk or meat for a time after the medicine is given, and during this time, neither meat nor milk should be used for human consumption. Check out www.uky.edu/Ag/AnimalSciences/goats/presentations/drugwithdrawtimeJan05.pdf for more information.

Some coughing is normal in goats. Especially if they're eating dry hay, you'll hear a cough now and then. Be concerned if it's a frequent or persistent cough, though. When goats are transported (to a show, to a new home, or on any trip), the stress of travel can trigger what's commonly called *shipping fever*, which is actually a form of pneumonia. Low copper levels depress immune function and make the goats more susceptible to upper-respiratory infections.

A persistent cough without an elevated temperature might indicate the presence of lungworms, a type of roundworm. If your goats have access to wet, undrained pasture, lungworms might be the cause because the intermediate hosts of lungworms are snails and slugs—critters who hang around in such environments. The diagnosis of lungworms is difficult, but the treatment is an adequate dose of Ivermectin, a wormer you might be using for other parasites anyway. (See Chapter 7 for more information about parasites, worming medicines, and worming.)

When a goat is running a fever, she feels bad and usually looks it. If her fever is elevated but she has no runny nose or coughing, look for other kinds of infection, even locally. See if she has a cut that's become infected. She may have a sticker, thorn, or sliver stuck somewhere that's causing the fever. Some other diseases can cause elevated temperatures, but they're not very common. You may need your vet for help in diagnosing.

Some goats have seasonal responses to dust, pollen, and nasal irritants that result in a runny nose. If your goat's temperature is normal but she has a nasal discharge, suspect an allergic reaction. Unlike humans, goats make their own vitamin C, but I've seen extra vitamin C given that cleared up allergic nasal symptoms in a couple days when nothing else helped. It's cheap, it's effective, and it has no side effects. Good medicine!

Vomiting

Goats vomit when they've eaten something toxic to them. Because it's so unlike their normal behavior, it can seem very alarming. In mild cases, just allow the goat to continue to get rid of what's causing the trouble. Unfortunately, you won't always know if it's mild or life-threatening. Look at the list of toxic plants at the end of Chapter 1. If you know you have any of those in the goat area, call your vet and get good medical advice about how to proceed.

It never hurts to get some activated charcoal into a vomiting goat. You can find activated charcoal at drug stores, pet stores, goat suppliers (look for Toxiban), and health-food stores. The dose is 500 grams suspended in liquid.

Diarrhea

Eighty percent of the time, diarrhea is caused by parasites. Most of the rest of the diarrhea is caused by goats getting into some kind of food they love and simply overeating.

There's another kind of diarrhea you should know about: if a baby goat under 3 weeks old has diarrhea, it's almost always caused by *E. coli* bacteria. Newborns can pick up *E. coli* through fecal matter in their pens. Treat *E. coli* with penicillin or penicillin-type drugs. It's curable if caught early.

If a baby goat over 3 weeks old gets diarrhea, it's almost certainly coccidia and should be treated with sulfa drugs. (See Chapter 7 for more about coccidia infections.)

Diarrhea in an adult is most often caused by overwhelming parasite problems. It should be diagnosed as to the type of parasite and treated with the appropriate worming medicine (three times at 10-day intervals). Remember that a sudden feed change, especially to rich alfalfa or new grass, can also cause diarrhea. Diarrhea is environmental or parasitic and almost never contagious.

The Eyes

Other than injury, the most common eye problem is pinkeye (Keratoconjunctivitis), a bacterial infection that makes eyes watery at first then reddish and swollen. It can cause blindness if not treated, and the sooner you start treatment, the less damage occurs. Pinkeye is highly contagious and can be spread by dust, flies, or contact, so if one of your goats has it, they probably all will.

Treatment for pinkeye is any of the tetracycline antibiotic injectables, LA-200, and Biomycin or Nuflor. Check with your medical adviser for dosage and frequency. Some people report using mastitis treatment and squirting the medicine directly into the eyes. Many brands of mastitis treatment come in tubes of antibiotic mixed with sesame oil.

The Skin

A fairly common skin complaint is little bumps all over the udder. They appear to be little pimples. Cow pox could cause such bumps, although I've never seen a case. It's more likely a staphylococcus bacterial infection, compounded by wet conditions like wet bedding and lots of rain. Clean up the wet areas where your goat might be lying. Clean the udder with a disinfectant wash, dry thoroughly with paper towels, and treat topically with mastitis treatment or any antibiotic cream. You can also use zinc oxide. The most common form of zinc oxide is generic diaper rash cream. Use sterile gloves when applying the cream so you don't add your own bacteria to the infected skin. This one isn't contagious, but is more about environment and immune function.

Another common skin complaint is crusty scabs, especially around the feet and lower legs, but they may also be around the tail, ears, sides of face, or belly. These are also common in wet conditions and on bucks where they wet themselves. The most common cause is a dermatophilus bacterial infection, also called strawberry foot rot, lumpy wool, and other names.

The bacteria are susceptible to many antibiotics, both topically and injected. If you want to be sure this is what you're dealing with, remove a scab and look at the underside. Dermatophilus scabs have hair follicles showing on the underneath side. Topical applications of antibiotic creams or mastitis medicines are more effective if the scabs are removed first. Severe cases may be painful but not life-threatening. Mild cases are unsightly and annoying, and the goat often ends up with bald patches. Surprisingly, this is not contagious.

Sore mouth lesions can end up on any location that the goat can touch with her muzzle. This is a viral infection and just has to run its course. It's more severe for very young kids who may stop eating because their mouths are so sore. Supportive care such as keeping them as comfortable as possible and hand feeding is the treatment. Once they've had it, they cannot get it again. It is very contagious. Use caution when treating sore mouth, as it can be contracted by humans.

Swelling

Some swelling, such as an injury, bump, or scrape, is self-explanatory. Some, however, is not so easy to decipher.

Mysterious bumps often have a not-so-mysterious sharp thing inside. Look for thorns, splinters, metal scraps, or a sharp tack. If something like that gets under the skin or into a hoof, the goat may get a localized infection that causes swelling. The fix is primarily about discovery and removal, and some goats may need treatment with antibiotics either topically or systemically.

Screwflies lay their eggs on moist or damaged goat skin, and the hatching larvae create a swelling where they feast on the goat's flesh. Technically, the United States eradicated the screwworm, but a case occasionally shows up. Screwworms are a reportable health problem, so check with your vet about treatment. Again, I'm a proponent of running your hand over your goats from head to tail once a day. It's a good way to catch small swellings before they become big problems.

In summer, maggots can be a problem in untreated injuries. Hydrogen peroxide is an easy treatment and will cause maggots to come out of the wound. Then spray the area with a wound spray product that will safely repel the flies, like Catron, Blu-Kote, or Red-Kote.

Bites can cause swelling whether the bite is from an insect, spider, or dog. You should know the poisonous insects or spiders in your area and how to treat for them. Your veterinarian is your best resource in such cases. Dog bites might cause swelling simply because there are so many bacteria in a dog's mouth. Clean any new open wounds with hydrogen peroxide, and clean minor punctures with soap and water. Treat swelling, tenderness, and redness with antibiotics. Penicillin is good against anaerobic microbes that cause infection in closed wounds.

Sometimes injection sites end up with a bump or a knot. These look worse than they are. They can occur when a Sub-Q shot gets *into* the layers of skin instead of *below* them, or because some medicines cause a reaction.

HERD HINT

I know that as I got better at giving shots over the years, my goats had fewer bumps. It's also one of the reasons I prefer giving shots in the loose skin over the ribs. Maybe it's easier to give shots correctly there or it's just a less-reactive area. These bumps can happen with IM shots as well.

In Chapter 3, I mentioned three diseases common in goats you should avoid when you're shopping for goats: caseous lymphadenitis (CL), caprine arthritis encephalitis (CAE), and parasites. All three can cause some swelling that is diagnostic.

CL creates abscesses around lymph nodes, especially in the face and neck, but sometimes in the shoulders and other body parts, too. There is no treatment for this disease other than lancing and cleaning the abscesses prior to their bursting. Avoid letting them burst at all costs.

CAE frequently presents as severe arthritis in the knees, which will then appear swollen. Severe symptoms may cause the goat to walk on her knees because of the pain. There is no cure for CAE, and it's spread through the milk and other bodily fluids of affected (even asymptomatic) goats who carry the virus. Because CAE affects milk production and other body systems, avoid bringing it onto your farm in the first place.

Last and most serious among swellings is a condition called Bottle Jaw, so named because the lower jaw becomes swollen. Bottle Jaw is the end result of a parasite infection so severe that it's life-threatening. The goat with Bottle Jaw is anemic and near death. Please don't allow parasites to get this out of control. Test and worm carefully, and see Chapter 7 for complete information on parasites.

Limping

Limping goats have sore feet, and there are two common causes for this, other than thorns and mechanical stickers.

The first is foot rot, a bacterial infection between the hoof wall and softer parts of the foot. It's more common among goats who need their feet trimmed and live under wet conditions. To treat, trim away the infected hoof wall, clean out the dirt and fecal matter that may be contributing, and treat with copper sulfate or zinc sulfate. In severe cases, a systemic antibiotic helps clear it up. Use long-acting penicillin or oxytetracycline (LA-200).

Goats are subject to laminitis (founder), just as horses are. The disease always follows a digestive upset such as getting into grain storage or rapid changes in feed. Laminitis causes inflammation and heat in the feet, damaging the blood supply to normal hoof tissue, and eventually causes the feet to grow at different rates in different areas. It's very painful, and the goat may refuse to stand or walk. Feel the normal hoof temperature on your goats, and if the hoof ever feels very hot, you're dealing with founder or laminitis. Quick first aid is to cool the feet by standing her in ice water, but you should also consult your vet to deal with this.

Coat Problems

The goat's coat is an indicator of her overall health. A healthy goat is sleek and shiny. One of the first indications of a health problem, often parasites, is hair that's wiry and dull or looks like it has split ends. The color of the hair is an indicator of copper levels. Low copper levels make the hair color fade. A severe deficiency can fade a colored goat to almost white. Sometimes the fading begins around the eyes. Copper deficiency also results in another hair anomaly—the tip of the tail goes bald.

Another coat problem is bald patches, which ringworm can cause. It's highly contagious and unsightly but not life-threatening at all. Once a goat has had ringworm, she will be immune forever. When the hair in the bald spot grows back, it may be a shade different. Ringworm can take several weeks or months to cycle through your entire herd, because it's very contagious.

Selective rubbing can also cause bald patches. It might indicate itchy skin, so check for skin parasites like mites and lice and be sure mineral levels are adequate. Zinc is especially important for skin health.

I cover copper supplementation at the end of this chapter because low copper contributes to and compounds all health problems and plays a role in all these factors that cause itching.

Udder and Milk Problems

An infection in the mammary glands of any mammal is called mastitis. Dairy animals such as cows and goats have extra stresses because of the milking process, and this makes them more vulnerable to mastitis. Cleanliness in milking is critical, and you need to be sure the goats have clean, dry bedding to lie down on after milking.

Many different organisms can cause an udder infection. Some organisms do permanent damage and are there for life. Some are more easily cured. Staph aureus is one of the worst and most prevalent. There are a few types of mastitis, like the gangrenous form, that are fatal. Prevention is far superior to treatment.

Any change in the "feel" of the goat's udder is an indication of possible problems. A normal udder is not overly hot and has no lumps within it. "Normal" means the halves are close to the same size and give close to the same amount of milk. Mastitis can cause visible changes in milk; it may appear stringy or watery. These occur more as the infection advances.

Once again, goats with high-normal copper and mineral levels are far more resistant to mastitis than if they are low. So it makes sense to ensure copper and mineral sufficiency. Be sure to milk at regular intervals, and don't allow a doe to overudder, which can also cause mastitis. Keeping udders clean and bedding dry is also good prevention. But there's a third strategy I recommend, called the California Mastitis Test (CMT). Available at suppliers and feed stores, CMT consists of a purple reagent you add to a small amount of milk and swirl around. If the milk thickens, it's an indication of infection in the milk. Testing frequently gives you a leg up on treatment should an infection get started. The milk can then also be cultured to determine what bacteria are there. Do not use any antibiotics before collecting a sterile milk sample for a culture.

You must collect the samples for culturing in a sterile manner. Squirt one stream of milk to clear the teat end and then swab the teat end with alcohol. Do not touch with your fingers; allow the alcohol to dry. It is only by drying that alcohol kills bacteria. Then, without allowing any paraphernalia or the edge of the tube to touch anything, squirt a little milk into a sterile tube or container, apply the cap, and ready it for the lab or freeze for later culturing.

KIDDING AROUND

One of the best websites about milk quality is www.uwex.edu/milkquality/index.html, sponsored by the University of Wisconsin.

To treat mastitis, you can use a tube of mastitis medicine (also used as treatments for skin problems). They have a blunt needlelike tip of plastic for inserting partway into the teat. Simply sterilize the teat tip, remove the covering from the tube tip, and keep all things from touching it that compromise sterility. When the teat tip is dry, line up the hole in the teat and the hole in the applicator, and inject the medicine into the udder. Don't insert the tip more than about ¼ inch. Follow label instructions for frequency of the infusion. Mastitis is environmental (especially copper deficiency) rather than contagious.

There are many brands of mastitis medicine and many different kinds of antibiotics. What you use depends on the bacteria your goat has. Check with your veterinarian. She can be invaluable help with this disease.

Sometimes milk in the bucket will have a slightly pink tinge to it. If it sits undisturbed in the jar for long, the pinkness settles to the bottom of the jar as a reddish layer. This is caused by mechanical trauma to the udder, more common in young, first-time milkers when the pressure of a full udder breaks a few capillaries inside the udder. The condition isn't serious and clears within a few days.

Milk from a mastitic udder contains pus. If milk ever looks or tastes wrong, discard it rather than allow your family to drink it. Milk with a bloody tinge can still be fed to goat kids.

Neurological Symptoms

The two main diseases causing neurological symptoms are tetanus and polio. If you remember from Chapter 7, tetanus organisms are ubiquitous on farms. The symptoms of tetanus begin with a stiff gait and an anxious-looking expression. Further along, the goat becomes rigid, lies flat on the ground with her legs extended, and will be sensitive to sound and light. Death is painful and ugly, usually occurring in 36 hours or less. The symptoms are very distinctive and hard to miss. If caught early, there is some possibility for recovery, but it takes heroic medicine and a knowledgeable vet.

Polio is short for polioencephalomalacia, a nutritional and metabolic disorder caused by lack of thiamin. It may follow a difficult weaning or an incident of getting too much to eat of goodies, like grain. Symptoms to watch for include listlessness, loss of appetite, and possibly diarrhea. Then the neurological symptoms begin: the goat holds her head too elevated, looking off into space, is very excitable, wanders aimlessly, circles, becomes blind, and eventually she'll be unable to get up, will have convulsions, and will die.

Recovery is probable with quick diagnosis and administration of injectable thiamin (by prescription). The dose is 4.5 ccs per 100 pounds of body weight of the 100/mg/ml strength of thiamin every 6 hours for 24 hours. Some have had success with large amounts of vitamin B complex (nonprescription) in the event you don't have thiamin on hand and cannot get it quickly. The dosage is the same.

Polio is sometimes confused with a disease called Listeriosis, or circling disease, which is bacterial and attacks the central nervous system. The treatment for Listeriosis is very high doses of penicillin in order to get levels high enough to cross the brain/blood barrier. If there's any question about which disease you're dealing with, treat for both and continue the treatment for 24 hours beyond when the symptoms cease.

When a Goat Goes Down

Many problems cause a goat to go down, including those issues mentioned in the earlier neurological category or something like advanced pneumonia. Any illness that progresses far enough could result in a down goat. Two other special situations are worth mentioning, however.

Ketosis

Ketosis is a metabolic disorder that occurs when a goat quits eating and starts burning her own body tissues (fats). Because it occurs when the goat stops eating, it's a secondary condition, meaning something else is causing a problem that makes her stop eating.

> **KIDDING AROUND**
>
> *Ketosis* is a term used much too often and many times incorrectly. *Pregnancy ketosis* is a misnomer. Pregnancy is one condition, and ketosis is a metabolic imbalance.

When a goat is burning her own body fat, it must be processed through the liver. The fats tend to build up, and the metabolites are released into the system, creating the characteristic acetone smell on the goat's breath. The accepted treatment is to raise the goat's glucose levels in some way, providing quick energy to enable the goat to stop living on her own body reserves. In mild cases, just providing delectable treats or molasses water might be enough. More severe cases, or when ketosis has been left untreated and becomes more severe, are sometimes treated with propylene glycol or intravenous glucose under your vet's supervision.

Ketosis is always secondary, so you must deal with the primary cause that made her stop eating. In many instances, it's a health problem that's made her feel really bad, like pneumonia. Treat that first, and then treat the ketosis.

Hypocalcemia

Another goat down situation occurs around the last stages of pregnancy or the first few weeks of lactation. The symptoms start with the goat's refusal to eat her grain and progresses to wobbly legs, shivering, failure of labor (depending on the stage of pregnancy), and then to a goat down and soon dead.

This very serious metabolic disorder goes by many names, most of them wrong. You may have heard of pregnancy toxemia, or milk fever. But it's neither a fever nor ketosis, although ketosis may also follow. The correct name is hypocalcemia, and it is a metabolic disease caused by an incorrect balance of calcium and phosphorus, usually not enough calcium compared to the phosphorus in the diet. This is a management problem caused by incorrect feeding.

Remember that grass, grass hay, and all grains are low in calcium and high in phosphorus. As a maintenance diet, goats can tolerate it fairly well. But when the demands of late pregnancy hit, the doe's need for calcium skyrockets so she can build her babies' bones and produce milk. When calcium needs are high but the diet is low, hypocalcemia results. Calcium is critical for muscle contractions. Labor and birth are a result of contractions of the muscular uterus. The heart is a muscle. Ultimately, in this disease, the heart stops beating, and death occurs.

HERD HINT

A temperature below normal (102°F) is highly diagnostic of a metabolic problem, and a temperature higher than normal (102°F to 103°F) indicates an infection. If the temperature is over 103°F, consider it a fever. If it's under 102°F, consider hypocalcemia, especially if it's near kidding time.

Prevention is better than treatment, because hypocalcemia puts tremendous stress on the heart over time, potentially shortening the goat's life span. Treatment is often too late to save either dam or kids. Prevention means that in high-demand times like the last third or even two thirds of pregnancy and the first few weeks of lactation her diet must contain enough calcium. Some alfalfa and not so much grain is a far better ration to keep kidding time trouble-free.

If somehow you've ended up with a doe showing symptoms of hypocalcemia, you need to get calcium into her. In mild cases, human calcium supplements might be all she needs. Change the diet. Feed her yogurt or milk. But in most cases, when people notice it's a problem, the goat is already in serious trouble. Often, the best treatment is intravenous calcium administered by a veterinarian. It's highly precarious, though, as too much calcium is as deadly as too little.

Another treatment that has saved many goats is administration of a drug called CMPK, given subcutaneously in large doses. CMPK is by prescription only but might be life-saving to have on hand. It is a solution of minerals (especially calcium) and glucose. The dosage for a full-size goat is 30 cc Sub-Q every two hours, day and night, until all danger is past. CMPK is usually refrigerated, so warm it to room temperature before administering it. There is also oral CMPK or MFO. It's dosed at the same rate. Be aware they may burn throat tissues.

Sue Reith has invented a kitchen recipe you can make using human mineral supplements. See the recipe at goats.wetpaint.com/page/Hypocalcemia+-+CMPK+Kitchen+Recipe. Consult with your veterinarian, and observe carefully for any recurrence of symptoms.

HERD HINT

If the treatment you use for any ailment isn't getting results (temperature coming down or improved appearance) within 24 to 36 hours, that's an indication you're not using the right treatment, so use something else. It's not unheard of to find that a particular antibiotic has no effect on the health problem you're trying to treat.

Antibiotics Commonly Used in Goats

Most veterinary (and some human) pharmaceuticals are not approved for use in goats and must be used off-label under the supervision of your veterinarian. Goats are considered a minor species, and few studies are done just for goats. Most research has been done on cattle, sheep, and swine. Nevertheless, many of the medicines for these other animals are also helpful for goat ailments. Goats tend to metabolize faster and may need larger or longer doses of some medicines than what the label suggests. Check with your veterinarian.

LA-200 (also Biomycin or Oxy-Shot) is a tetracycline antibiotic. Available at most feed stores, it's one of the cheapest and most often used antibiotics for treating pinkeye, hoof rot, pneumonia, metritis, and mastitis. The recommended dosage is 4.5 cc per 100 pounds of body weight, given Sub-Q, preferably with a 1-inch by 20-gauge needle. Give one repeat injection 48 to 72 hours after the first. It may sting.

Penicillin is one of the oldest antibiotics and is used in specific situations—some pneumonias and closed wounds. It has been severely overused and may not be as effective as it once was. It's available at most feed stores. The recommended dosage is 5 cc per 100 pounds of body weight for five consecutive days, and it must be stored in the refrigerator in the meantime. Penicillin G Benzathine, a long-acting penicillin, is also available. Check with your veterinarian for dosage and usage.

Naxcel or Excenel (ceftiofur sodium) are two versions of a broad-spectrum antibiotic used primarily for upper-respiratory illnesses such as pneumonia. Naxcel or Excenel can also be used to treat metritis (post-kidding uterine infection). It's available by prescription only. Naxcel comes as a dry powder that must be reconstituted with sterile water before use. Once the product is liquefied, it will only keep seven days in the refrigerator, but you can draw it into individual syringes and freeze it for up to a month or more. Excenel is much easier to use because it's a premixed liquid and can be kept at room temperature. Excenel is a fairly thick liquid and is best given in an 18-gauge needle. The recommended dosage to treat pneumonia is 2 cc per 100 pounds of body weight once every 24 hours for three days. The recommended dosage to treat metritis (uterine infections) is 2 cc per 100 pounds of body weight every 24 hours for five days. Both are prescription-only products.

Nuflor (Florfenicol) is another broad-spectrum antibiotic used for hard-to-treat infections. Nuflor can be administered as a large single dose Sub-Q, or two smaller IM doses 24 hours apart. The recommended dosage is 6 cc per 100 pounds of body weight for the one-time Sub-Q dose, or 3 cc per 100 pounds of body weight for the IM doses. Dosage for kids is 1 cc per 25 pounds once every 24 hours for two doses. Available by prescription only, Nuflor is best given with an 18-gauge needle.

Biosol (Neomycin Sulfate), available at most feed stores, is used for treating bacterial scours. The recommended dosage is 5 cc per 100 pounds, orally.

Gentamycin is an antibiotic spray used for treating pinkeye and is available at most feed stores.

Albon (Sulfadimethoxine) is a sulfa antibiotic used to treat coccidiosis, but it can also be used to treat pneumonia, foot rot, and other bacterial infections. At the 12.5 percent strength available at most feed stores (a clear, very bitter-tasting liquid), the dosage is 1 cc per 5 pounds of body weight the first day, followed by 1 cc per 10 pounds of body weight daily for four more days. At the 5 percent strength often found at vet clinics (a thick yellow liquid that smells like peppermint or bananas), the dosage is 5 ccs per 10 pounds of body weight the first day, and 5 ccs per 20 pounds of body weight for days two through five. It can be given undiluted or mixed in a kid's individual bottle of milk.

To-Day (cephapirin sodium) is used to treat mastitis while a doe is in milk. It's available at most feed stores and supply houses. Milk out her udder completely before infusing the medication, and use one tube per side, taking care to insert the syringe only as far into the teat canal as necessary (¼ to ½ inch). Before infusing, carefully clean each teat with the alcohol swab included in the box of medication and allow it to air-dry. A small amount of milk should be expressed into a clean blood tube (one tube for each teat). Refrigerate or freeze samples for a bacterial culture later if your treatment of choice does not work.

After infusing each side of the udder, squeeze near the end of the teat to close it off without touching the orifice, and gently massage the medication up into the udder itself. Repeat this treatment 12 hours later. If the mastitis has not cleared up after the second treatment, take the sterile milk sample you saved to your vet and have it cultured. Systemic antibiotics can be given in conjunction with infusions. Some use tetracycline antibiotics for its longest withdrawal time; others use Naxcel or Excenel.

Tomorrow (cephapirin sulfate) is the antibiotic udder infusion used when drying up a doe. It's available at feed stores and supply houses. Use one tube in each side of the udder when you are no longer milking the doe and her udder has begun to go dry. Completely milk out each side before treating, use sterile procedures, and do not milk again until the doe freshens after kidding.

Pirsue (pirlimicin hydrochloride) is another antibiotic udder infusion used to treat mastitis caused by staph and strep bacteria. It's only available by prescription. The usual treatment is one tube in each side of the udder, followed by a second application 24 hours later, just as with To-Day, discussed earlier. The goat should be milked at regular 12-hour intervals. Pirsue appears to be very effective in treating cases of subclinical mastitis, where the only indication that something is wrong is a drop in milk production in one side of the udder.

GOAT HORN

Micotil is an antibiotic commonly used for respiratory infections in cattle. *Never* use Micotil on goats because it kills goats (and horses). Some veterinarians are not aware of Micotil's potential toxicity to goats.

When a Goat Dies

Sometimes a goat dies, and sometimes you must put down a very sick goat. If you're going to have your veterinarian euthanize your sick goat, he will often dispose of the carcass for you, although there may be a charge.

If a goat dies for unknown reasons, it might be smart to take the carcass to your vet for an autopsy because discovering the cause of death may help you prevent another. If an animal dies at your place and you have the land for it, you can bury the carcass.

Or check in your area for pet crematoriums or rendering plants. Or ask around for someone who will pick up the carcass. Look at www.hsus.org/horses_equines/resources for information organized by states. This is for horses but probably applies equally well to other species.

The Least You Need to Know

- You need to learn how to assess symptoms and temperature because they can help you pinpoint what's wrong with your goat.
- A runny nose or coughing indicates an upper respiratory infection.
- Vomiting indicates poisoning, and diarrhea can have several causes.
- Pinkeye is the most common eye infection, but the skin can have many problems that require unique treatments.
- Swelling can indicate a mechanical, viral, or bacterial infection, and limping is usually about foot rot, a bacterial infection in wet conditions.
- Hair reflects overall health, and therefore can be diagnostic of more serious problems like mineral deficiencies.
- The udder can get an infection called mastitis, and prevention is invaluable because such infections are sometimes impossible to cure.
- Neurological symptoms are almost always about tetanus or goat polio.

Producing and Using Goat Milk

In This Chapter

- How to milk your goats
- The importance of cleanliness
- Proper milk handling and storage
- The nutritional benefits of goat milk
- What else you can do with goat milk

Goat milk is a main reason why some people decide to get goats. If that sounds like you, good for you! You're going to have quite an adventure. There are thousands of goat-milk lovers in the United States, but there are *millions* around the world. With just a little care and practice, you can be drinking nature's perfect food.

In this chapter, I start by explaining the mechanics of getting milk from the goat and into the pail. That's important, of course. But then I want to lead you through some of the finer details of goat milk care and use.

The Mechanics of Milking

Milking is a simple skill, but you'll need to practice. Many of us practiced on goats until we "got" it. That works well *if* the goat is a patient one and you have plenty of time. Remember, the goat fills her udder twice a day, and with a full udder there is some urgency to empty it. When at all possible, practice on someone else's goats—preferably someone who will both teach you and take over for you when you get tired.

The activity of milking uses muscles in your hands and forearms. These muscles don't get much use in your daily activities, so your hands *will* get tired. These muscles may even get sore, as newly exercised muscles tend to do. To build up strength for milking, you can squeeze a small ball or a hand exerciser.

Think of the goat's udder system generally as a balloon with valves that open under pressure. The openings are called the *orifices*, and one is found at the end of each teat. The average udder has two teats with one orifice each. (Anything else is a cull goat.) To milk, you need to close off the top of the teat between your straight thumb and the lowest knuckle of your index finger, where it connects to the body of the udder. You'll use a pinching action to close off the milk in the teat and keep it from returning to the reservoir of the udder. Once you've closed the milk in the teat, you apply pressure with your other four fingers, squeezing the body of the teat, to squeeze the milk out of the orifice. Release the pinching finger so more milk flows down into the teat and repeat.

There's a lot of variation in the size of both the teats and the orifices. Longer teats are easier to get a grip on, and larger orifices take less pressure to squeeze the milk from. The position of the teats on the udder floor also makes a difference. Teats that point straight down instead of outward make hitting a bucket easier.

These are all things to consider when choosing milk goats. If you're a well-practiced milker, these things may not be an issue. But for beginners, less-than-ideal teat placement and small orifices will slow you down and might make it more difficult for you to learn.

You can practice the basic move ahead of time on a partially inflated balloon or rubber glove. Obviously, there are some differences, but you can get your hands used to the basic mechanical movement.

Keeping It Clean

Milk is the most perfect medium for bacterial growth. Bacteria *love* milk. Bacteria ruin milk quality. And some bacteria can make you or even your goats sick. So you can probably see why cleanliness is priority one.

Let's look at three areas where cleanliness is of the utmost importance—in the goat yard, with the milk, and with the udder.

Both you and your goats will have a better milking experience if cleanliness is one of your priorities in all these areas.

Cleanliness in the Goat Yard

The most open part of the goat's milk-producing system is on the underneath side of her, and that area comes in contact with the goat yard surface every time she lies down. The cleaner everything is, the less chance for problems.

The process of milking a goat causes a bit more stress on the orifice than when kids nurse. Studies in the cow dairy industry indicate that the orifice stretches and remains somewhat open for up to an hour after milking. If she goes directly into the goat yard and lies down after milking, that open orifice can allow bacteria to get inside.

The risk can be lowered by making sure her bedding is dry and as clean as you can keep it. Avoid wet, soggy, high-fecal-content bedding. Some goat owners optimize the time after milking by feeding hay then so the goats are standing to eat for about an hour. Or if your goats go out to browse or graze after milking, you'll get a similar effect.

Cleanliness with the Milk

Bacteria in the milk will grow and multiply. They change the taste, making it "goaty," a taste I can't begin to describe, but one you'd recognize if you tasted it. Bacteria cause milk to sour. Very clean milk will keep for 10 days or longer in the refrigerator and still be great for drinking. Anything you can do to keep bacterial counts low gives you better milk.

You'll have better luck keeping your milking area clean if it's separate from where the goats normally live. Enclosing your milk room also helps with cleanliness. It keeps insects and weather out and dust down.

Your climate may determine some of the details of your milk room. I've had many types of milk rooms and can tell you that there's no one correct kind. Some milk rooms are within barns; others are stand-alone. Some are stainless and tile; others are rough lumber with odds and ends. Only you know what works best for you.

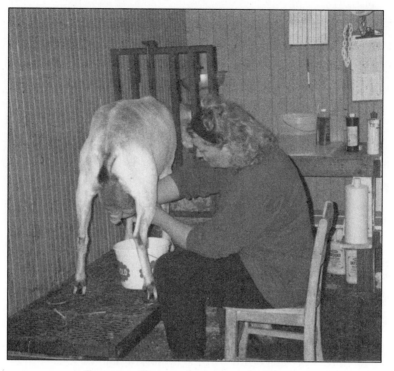

Create a milk room that's convenient for you.

Cleanliness of the Udder

Think about the position of the goat's udder relative to the milk bucket. It's directly above it, right? Obeying the law of gravity, any debris on the udder or its immediate surroundings may fall and land in your bucket. Debris is covered with bacteria, which then can get into the milk. That's counterproductive to getting good-quality milk.

Brushing the hair and udder to remove debris before milking helps keep everything clean. The dairy clip (remember that from Chapter 5?) helps further reduce debris.

Not only for clean milk, but also to reduce risk of udder problems, prior to milking you should wash the udder. Wash with a damp (not dripping!) paper towel or single-use cloth using warm water and a mild detergent such as liquid dish soap. Washing solutions are also commercially available.

Be sure the towel or cloth is damp only, not dripping! Bacteria-laden water running down to the ends of the teats just puts more bacteria at the most vulnerable point of the udder.

You should also use a *strip cup*. The first squirt of milk goes into the strip cup rather than the bucket. The first squirt of milk contains more bacteria and doesn't help milk quality, so don't put that in with the rest of the milk in the bucket. And if there are any preliminary changes in the milk, the strip cup can show them before you get a whole bucketful.

It's helpful to use a *teat dip* after milking, too. A teat dip helps keep bacteria out of the orifice for that hour or so after milking when it's most vulnerable. Teat dips are available commercially in a variety of antibiotic or disinfecting chemicals, preparations, and applicators. Various studies show mixed results for teat dips made with iodine, so you'll have to figure out what works best for you.

DEFINITION

A **strip cup** is a small container with a screen attached that filters the first squirt of milk. If there are any lumps, clots, or anomalies, they'll be visible on the screen. **Teat dip** is an antibacterial liquid dipped or sprayed onto teat ends to reduce the chances of bacteria getting into the udder.

Cooling and Storing Milk

You've milked the goat, and you have a bucket of milk. Now what? You strain it. Single-use milk filters are a good investment to remove any debris that inadvertently got into the bucket.

Try several setups of filter, strainer, or your own tools until you find what's comfortable for you. Whether you opt for a commercially available strainer from a goat supplier or use a funnel with a milk filter inside, do what works for you.

Strain the milk into very clean containers that make sense for your family. Glass is easiest to keep clean, and canning jars such as Kerr, Mason, and others are readily available in 1- and 2-quart sizes. You might even be able to purchase new plastic milk containers from dairy supply stores, often locally.

Once the milk is in the jar, you need to get it cold as fast as possible. Some people put it in a freezer for a while. If it stays in there too long, of course, you may have frozen milk or, if you poured the milk in glass, you might have broken containers. A safer and actually more effective cooling method is to set the milk in an icy water bath until it's chilled. Then refrigerate the milk at the coldest refrigerator temperature available. Grade A milk must be stored at 40°F or below, by law. That includes your milk, too! You'll be even happier with the taste and longevity if you cool it to 38°F. Never pour warm milk directly into "cold" milk from a previous milking. It can boost bacterial growth and shorten your milk's shelf life.

Really clean goat milk stored at temperatures cooler than 40°F will keep for a week or longer without changes in taste. Milk with a high bacteria count will begin to taste "goaty" in just a few days and will sour very quickly.

Goat Milk Is Good for You

Goat milk is remarkably similar to cow's milk. It contains protein, lipids (milk fat), vitamins, minerals, and water. That's where the similarities end, however, in the composition of the fats, protein, and amounts of vitamins and minerals.

Goat milk contains vitamin A (which is colorless) instead of the *carotenoids* cow's milk contains. *Carotenes* are the yellow pigment that colors cow's milk butter and natural cheese. Carotenes convert to vitamin A for most people (but not for diabetics). What does this mean for your goat milk and its products? It will all be stark white.

DEFINITION

Carotenes are the precursors of vitamin A. These colorful compounds give carrots their orange color and are found in many fruits and vegetables. **Carotenoids** are a group of carotenes from the green things the cow or goat eats. Goats convert that compound to colorless vitamin A; cows do not.

The fat in goat milk has several differences from the fat in cow's milk. The fat globules are smaller, which makes them stay suspended longer in the milk. Goat milk is also missing an agglutinin, a compound that makes fat tend to clump faster in cow's milk. These factors make goat milk more "homogenized" than cow's milk and contribute to its digestibility. Some cream will rise if goat milk is left undisturbed in the refrigerator overnight, but it's not anything like the cream that rises in raw cow's milk.

Mechanically homogenized cow's milk, where the fat globules are forced through a screen, does mimic the natural homogenization of goat milk. It also, unfortunately, releases an enzyme associated with milk fat called xanthine oxidase, which then travels through the digestive membranes into the bloodstream. Once there, it behaves like a free radical, scarring heart and blood vessels. The body's defense is to lay down protective cholesterol, or plaque. This effect is not found from naturally homogenized goat milk, or even raw cow's milk. Without mechanical homogenization, xanthine oxidase is not released and is naturally excreted.

Another difference in goat milk fat is that it contains more short- and medium-chain fatty acids. These are more easily burned as fuel rather than stored as fat in your body, and it makes a softer fat that's healthier for you.

The protein in goat milk is missing the most common casein of cow's milk, alpha-s-1 casein, which is also the protein causing many allergic reactions to cow's milk. Most people who are allergic to cow's milk proteins can easily tolerate goat milk. This protein difference is also the reason cheese-making is significantly different with goat milk.

Along with the vitamin A difference, goat milk is higher in B vitamins than cow's milk, especially niacin, except for B_6 and B_{12}. It's higher in minerals, too, especially calcium, phosphorus, magnesium, and manganese, but lower in sulfur, iron, and zinc.

One more difference: goat milk is lower in lactose, or milk sugar, although the difference is minor. Nevertheless, people with lactose intolerance are often able to tolerate goat milk.

People who live in the world's "blue zones"—where longevity is the rule, not the exception—most often drink goat milk. This implies that goat milk might be part of the reason for their extraordinary longevity. Many anecdotal stories exist of great improvements in health when people start drinking goat milk.

Goat milk's better digestibility extends beyond human consumption. It's also easier for almost all animals to digest and is used for orphans of all kinds and sizes.

KIDDING AROUND

Calves can tolerate amounts of goat milk that would cause diarrhea if it were cow's milk. I once raised a Holstein calf with extra goat milk, and when I sold him at weaning, the buyer commented that he looked better than a calf his age had any right to look! I've also raised and provided goat milk for orphans of many other species, including cats, dogs, opossums, foals, sheep, baby birds, mice, ferrets, llamas, alpacas, and large felines.

Goat Milk–Based Products

If you like milk, you'll love drinking a glass of clean and cold goat milk. It tastes similar to good cow's milk, but *better*. (Okay, I'm biased here, but I think you'll soon agree with me after a few glasses.) Drinking the milk comes at the top of the list of favorite uses for goat milk. For many people, the second and third spots go to cheese and butter. The French call the cheese *chèvre*, which is the French word for "goat." Americans have in part picked up that name.

Goat Milk Cheese

Making elaborate cheeses with your goat milk is beyond the scope of this book, although I've included two great cheese-making books in Appendix B you can check out if you like. You can make any variety of cheese with goat milk that you can make with other milks.

Don't believe me? Check out this quick and easy soft goat cheese recipe. You don't need any special skills or equipment beyond a candy thermometer and a stainless-steel pot.

Quick and Easy Soft Goat Cheese

This soft, spreadable cheese may remind you a little of cream cheese or ricotta. It's very mild and picks up the flavors of any additives.

Yield:
1 to 1½ quart cheese

1 gal. goat milk
¼ cup vinegar or lemon juice

1. Pour goat milk into a stainless-steel pan or a double boiler and set over very low heat. (Use any extra milk you have and adjust the recipe to match the amount.) Milk scorches easily, so heat to 145°F over very low heat, or use a double boiler. If using a double boiler, you can heat over high heat to 145°F.

2. Turn off the heat, and add vinegar. Stir thoroughly but briefly.

3. Allow milk to cool, undisturbed, for up to 2 hours or more.

4. When milk is cool or at room temperature, cut or stir curd and pour into a colander lined with sterile, wide-weave cloth such as cheesecloth or pieces of old sheets or cotton clothing that's been sterilized. Allow to drain over the sink for 1 to 4 hours.

5. Mix in any seasonings or flavorings you like. Garlic powder, sea salt, dried herbs, and packaged ranch salad dressing powder are all favorites. Try dried fruit or canned pineapple, a little smoke flavor, granola, or anything else you can think of.

6. Pack in airtight containers and refrigerate. This soft, spreadable cheese will keep for only a few days in the refrigerator, but it freezes well.

Variation: You can adjust this recipe and make a firmer cheese by heating the milk to 180°F and then following the recipe as directed. This firmer cheese will last up to 2 weeks in your refrigerator, and it slices more like a dry Colby.

Goat Milk Butter

Goat milk butter is difficult to make in large quantities without a separator, but you can make small amounts using this no-equipment method.

Goat Milk Butter

This delicious, rich butter tastes just like any butter you've ever eaten, but it looks very different.

Yield:
varies

Fresh goat milk
Salt

1. Pour fresh milk into small-neck bottles—1- or 2-quart jars work well. Refrigerate overnight without disturbing.

2. The next day, remove the bottles from the refrigerator and, using a large metal spoon, carefully skim out as much as you can of the cream that's risen to the top. Place the cream in a clean quart jar, and freeze. Repeat each day while you collect more cream.

3. When the jar of cream is about half full, remove it from the freezer and let it come to room temperature.

4. Begin shaking the jar back and forth. Milk fat (butter) will begin to clump out of the other liquid (sweet buttermilk) after enough shaking, depending on the temperature and the vigor with which you shake. (Feel free to set down the jar and rest whenever you need a break.)

5. When you have a distinct clump of butter sloshing around with the liquid, drain off the liquid and place the butter in a clean bowl that is much larger than the clump of butter.

6. Wash the butter in cold running water, pressing it repeatedly with a spoon, rubber spatula, or other utensil. Keep pressing it under running water until the water runs clear and is no longer cloudy.

7. Add salt to taste, mixing it in thoroughly.

You'll notice that your goat butter is pure white—that's normal! Be sure to keep it refrigerated. Goat milk butter tends to be very soft—practically a puddle!—at room temperature.

KIDDING AROUND

You can make great yogurt from goat milk. Any other product made wholly or partly from cow's milk can easily be made using goat milk. Try substituting in any recipe you like.

What Should I Do with Extra Milk?

A goat's lactation has peaks and valleys, and at times you'll probably have more milk than you can comfortably use. A normal lactation period for the dairy breeds is 305 days, and depending on the goat, she could be giving twice or three times the amount of milk at the beginning than at the end. If you have more milk than you can use at times, you're not alone. But what should you do with it?

Selling your extra goat milk might be an option, depending on what state you live in. Check out realmilk.com to see if selling milk is legal in your state.

If it's not legal to sell milk for human consumption in your state, you still might be able to sell it for pets and orphans. Check for labeling requirements in your state, and market to vets, zoos, and people who rescue and raise alpacas, racehorses, big cats, etc.

If you decide to use your extra goat milk to raise other animals at your place, you can certainly enhance and serve your family's lifestyle. Raising a beef calf on goat milk makes for some great beef—or some extra income. Many people with extra goat milk use it to raise pigs. Milk-fed pork is some of the best-tasting pork. Many breeders raise an extra pig to sell, creating more family income.

You can also preserve your extra milk for a time when fresh milk won't be available. Freezing is one easy option. The faster you freeze fresh milk, and the closer it stays to 0°F, the better it will be when it thaws. If your frozen milk separates when it thaws, which sometimes happens, shake it vigorously until it reconstitutes.

For about the last 100 years, people have been preserving milk by canning it in regular or wide-mouth canning jars. Many people still do.

GOAT HORN

The U.S. Department of Agriculture now cautions that milk and milk products should not be canned because milk is a low-acid food and could possibly host botulism if not canned correctly. Botulism kills. If you decide to preserve milk in this way, be aware of this potential danger.

Goat milk soap and other skin-care products using goat milk is a growing cottage industry across the United States in recent years. Goat milk makes a product that's especially healthful for skin care and really enhances cleansing and moisturizing properties. Goat milk soap consists of goat milk, lye, and various oils and fragrances. It sometimes contains botanicals or other ingredients for specialized functions, such as exfoliating, to dry oily skin, for color, for texture, or just for fun.

If you're interested in making goat milk soap or other products, see Chapter 10 or check out Appendix B, where I list books on making goat milk soap.

There are also tremendously helpful websites about making soap, with many suppliers of soap-making ingredients providing tips and recipes as well as the ingredients and equipment. Simply Google "soap ingredient suppliers" or "fragrance suppliers" or "lye soap ingredients" for a start. I find the soaps with a high percentage of olive oil make the finest soaps, but experiment with your own recipes.

The Least You Need to Know

- Getting the milk out of the goat is a simple mechanical process, but beware: it uses muscles you might not be used to using!

- Keeping goat milk clean takes effort and attention, but it rewards you with great-tasting milk that keeps for many days at 40°F or cooler.

- Keeping the barn, milking area, and goat's udder clean protects the goat from udder infections and helps ensure good-quality milk. Cooling and storing the milk correctly also ensures safety and great taste.

- Goat milk is more digestible and nutritious because its composition is different from cow's milk.

- Goat milk is outstanding for drinking; for making butter, cheese, yogurt, and goat milk soap; and for feeding to orphaned animals or other livestock.

What Else Can Goats Do for You?

Chapter

10

In This Chapter

- The fun of showing your goats
- Goat meat, leather, and fertilizer
- Carting and packing with goats
- The educational and commercial potential of goats
- The intangibles goats bring

By now you've probably realized how remarkable goats are. They provide fresh, delicious products for your family as well as tons of cuteness and enjoyment. But there are even more things your goats can do for you! Some of them require a lot of work on your part, but each has its own appeal. Depending on how much time you have, whether or not you have children at home, and what your level of creativity is, some of the activities and products in this chapter might be something to add to your goat to-do list.

Should you decide somewhere along the way that you'd like goats to create some income for you, there are possibilities for that, too. I cover some of those in this chapter.

Showing Your Goats

If you've got a strong competitive bent, goat shows might be for you. If you started with registered animals with good conformation, they may be very worthy of competition. Nearly every breed registry sponsors shows. Dairy breeds probably have the most well-defined protocols and more shows available, but if you have other kinds of goats, look into the show possibilities for them as well.

Even if you don't have the best animals, showing is a way to get a judge's opinion. This can be valuable for new breeders to learn what in their animals needs improvement. Showing is also a way to forge long-lasting friendships and is a very social activity.

A goat show is also a venue perfect for children to participate in. I've seen children as young as 3 or 4 showing goats and doing a passable job. Judges and other competitors tend to cut them a little slack on showmanship because everyone realizes it's a learning and confidence-building experience, even in the very young. They also realize these young exhibitors are the future of the goat industry!

These teenagers are setting up their goats in a show.

Most goat shows have pens where the goats are stabled until their appearance in the show ring. There's a judge who's knowledgeable about the conformation and appearance of the breeds in the show. Each goat competes against other goats of their breed and of the same approximate age in classes. The goats are expected to walk around the show ring to be evaluated while on the move. Then they are asked to stand still in a particular way, called *setup*. Usually the judge gets his hands on the goats to determine how well they conform to the standard.

When the judge has assessed all the goats in a class, he'll point out the order in which he wants them to line up, beginning with the choice of first place. The judge then explains why he has placed them in that order, giving *reasons* that correspond to the scorecard for the breed. Listening to the reasons can be a great learning experience for people who are just learning about good goat conformation.

> **DEFINITION**
>
> **Setup** is the position a goat should be in while she's being judged in a show ring. The goats must place their legs evenly, have their head up, and have their back nice and straight. In other words, the goat should look her best and be alert and radiant! **Reasons** are what the judge talks about to justify the placings in a class.

After a goat has placed first in her class, she is expected to compete with all the other first-place animals for grand champion. There's always both a junior and a senior grand champion if there are junior and senior animals in the show. Then if the show contains more than one breed, the grand champions in each breed compete against each other for the designation of best in show.

There can be a lot of satisfaction in winning any of the classes, and even more in winning grand champion or best in show. It says you're serious about good goats, that you have a good breeding program, and that if people buy goats from you, the chances are good that they'll also get good goats. If that kind of competition appeals to you, then goat shows might be a fun activity in your future!

Goat Meat and Leather

Not everyone wants to eat goat meat, especially if your goats become your pets. Nevertheless, goat meat is delicious, and it's the meat most commonly eaten in the world. It tastes a little like lamb but is considerably leaner.

Getting a goat butchered might be more feasible and easier if there's a mobile butchering service in your area or if you know someone who's competent and not squeamish about the process. In my experience, people who are hunters are usually willing to do the butchering.

If you choose to do your own butchering, it's important to do it in the most humane way. Because of the thick bone on the front of a goat's head, the best place to shoot one is in the back of the head or just below the ear, pointing into the brain area. Put a little grain on the ground, and while he eats, place your gun just below the horns on the back of the head. No one enjoys butchering, but attention to correct procedure makes it quick and painless. That's the least we can offer these animals who serve us in life and after. For more information and photos that show the details of butchering, see the website tiny.cc/CAG0k.

Cook meat from young goats as you would lamb or almost any other red meat. If the animal is 4 to 8 weeks of age, the meat is called *cabrito*. For meat from older animals, called *chevon*, you may need to cook it slower, covered, or with liquid. Because it's so lean, goat meat tends to lose moisture and get tough. You can marinate it in wine or other marinades. Chevon is often barbecued, baked, or stewed.

DEFINITION

Cabrito is meat from animals between 4 and 8 weeks of age—in other words, it's milk-fed. **Chevon** is the designation for meat from animals older than 8 weeks.

If you have goat meat, you'll likely have the goat hides to deal with. You've heard of kid-skin gloves, but did you ever consider making them? Making leather from your own hides is a labor-intensive project, and not everyone wants to do it. But there's something pretty amazing about putting in the time and effort to create leather or buckskin from a goat hide. I've made buckskin out of deer hides, elk hides, and goat hides, and I can tell you, goat is qualitatively softer and drapes differently from the others.

You might not be up for the work of making leather, and that's fine. But rather than just throw away the hides, try to find someone who does like to make leather or buckskin. Muzzleloader clubs and Buckskinner organizations are full of people who might be interested in your hides, for money or for barter. See www.crazycrow.com/links_muzzle/associations.php for lists of these organizations.

If you change your mind and decide to try making your own leather, find information about how to do it online or check your local library for books on tanning leather and buckskin.

The Poop on Fertilizer

If you have goats, you'll have manure that accumulates, especially in the areas where goats congregate. If you leave it indefinitely, the manure will get deep and you'll eventually have severe fly and parasite problems. Not good. So what do you do with it?

The easiest thing to do with excess manure is pile it in a little used area where it can sit undisturbed for a year to compost. After about a year, you have a fertilizer that's wonderful to use in gardens, flower beds, around fruit trees, and anywhere good, organic nutrients will help.

Fertilizer provides three main plant nutrients—nitrogen, phosphorus, and potassium, known as NPK on fertilizer labels. In doing research on goat fertilizer, I found analysis of goat fertilizer that varied widely. The actual numbers of NPK for goat fertilizer only matters if you live in a state where fertilizer is strictly regulated and you want to sell it commercially. For your own use or for sharing with friends who garden, just be aware that it makes for a wonderful garden and great gardening!

Putting the Goat Before the Cart

Goats have been used for pulling carts for thousands of years—the earliest evidence of goat carts is about 4,000 years old. Goats can actually help you do some work at your place or pull people in the carts. Plus, a goat pulling a cart is so out of the ordinary that it creates great interest with the public. A goat and a cart can be used to draw attention to anything you want to promote and publicize. Goats and carts are a welcome addition to parades and other public celebrations.

Goats are very good at pulling carts.
(Elise Anderson)

The goats best suited to pulling a cart are wethers, the neutered males. The full-size boys do very well at pulling a cart and some of the cross-breed goats do well, too, even though they're smaller.

Training a goat to pull a cart takes a lot of time, patience, and some effort. Start before he gets full grown, using no weight or very light weights in the cart until he gets used to it and grows into a full-grown adult.

Pony carts tend to be too big and heavy for goats, but dog carts usually work well. Halters are usually used for goats rather than bridles with a bit. You can buy harnesses and carts, but you can also make your own. The Internet has many sites that show carts, harnesses, and bridle arrangements as well as dozens of websites that discuss training methods. Remember to be patient and enjoy the process.

Remember, too, that goats like to follow you, not lead. When attached to a cart, they need to be led around for some time until they catch on that they're supposed to be pulling the cart.

Check Appendix B for a list of cart and pulling equipment suppliers, many of which extensively discuss training on their sites.

Putting Your Goats to Work: Packing

You might think only mules and horses are good pack animals, but goats can carry a pack, too, and are great porters for wilderness trips where pack animals are permitted. Plus, they have a smaller carbon footprint than horses, mules, or burros because their feet do less damage and their manure isn't as intrusive.

Goats can carry about 25 percent of their own body weight as adults and possibly up to a third of their body weight if they're very large and in excellent condition. Determine how much a goat weighs by using a *weigh tape* available at any of the goat suppliers listed in Appendix B. To use the tape, measure around the goat's rib cage just behind the front legs. That measure will tell you how much the goat weighs.

DEFINITION

A **weigh tape** is a measuring tape that relates the size around the goat's midsection to the goat's weight for accurate dosing or determining how much weight the goat could carry. **Panniers** are the bags or baskets that attach to the saddle pack goats wear. Panniers hold your supplies and gear for a pack trip.

An adult goat can carry about 20 to 30 percent of her body weight in a pack.
(Nathaniel Kemper)

Several types of tack are available for pack goats. The crossbuck saddle is made of wood (with an angle of 86 degrees that fits most goats well) and is similar to those used on pack horses. Lighter versions are made of aluminum. For young goats or for a light load, there's a soft pack that doesn't need a saddle. *Panniers* are the bags or baskets that attach to the saddle and hold your stuff. Check Appendix B for a list of websites for pack equipment suppliers.

Training goats to carry a pack involves getting them used to following, being tied when appropriate, crossing streams and creeks, wearing the saddle, and then carrying weight. Like training to pull a cart, training goats to carry a pack takes time and patience. You can find more information about training in an online manual by Escape Goats at www.utahpackgoats.com and several of the supplier websites. The definitive book is John Mionczynski's *Pack Goats* (see Appendix B).

Fun with Goats in 4-H and FFA

4-H is a youth organization devoted to helping young adults be active and positive members of society and is usually associated with rural projects, values, and activities. The four H's of 4-H are head, heart, hands, and health. It is associated with the county extension services, and extension agents often coordinate some of the 4-H activities like the competitions at the county fair.

Regular 4-H membership begins when children are 8 years old and continues through high school. There are often special subsidiaries for younger children, although they are excluded from the competitions of regular 4-H until age 8. Each 4-H member is required to have a project each year, and although livestock isn't the only possibility, it's a project many children tackle.

FFA, or Future Farmers of America, is an organization for middle school and high school students and focuses on agricultural education. Each member must have at least one livestock- or agricultural-related project each year, such as planning the operation of an agricultural-related business.

Goats are a great answer to the projects required by both 4-H and FFA. Each organization has goat shows their members participate in. While other livestock projects are sometimes chosen, goats are uniquely suitable and desirable. Their size makes them easy to handle even for younger children, and they learn important values from the care and management of goats.

The children compete in showmanship, which includes the *fitting* of the animal— how good the goat looks, how well they handle their goat in the show ring, and how close to the uniform standards the exhibitor appears. They also compete in *open classes*, in which the goat is judged on her conformation and faithfulness to the standard for her breed.

DEFINITION

Fitting is the process of preparing a goat for show and includes clipping her hair, cleaning her, and trimming her hooves. (Males are rarely fitted.) **Open classes** are all about the goat's conformation and appearance as opposed to showmanship classes, which are partly about the exhibitors' skill and appearance, although having showmanship skills can give an exhibitor an advantage in showing the goat to its best advantage.

Making Goat Milk Soap

If you like the idea of making goat milk soap for your family, you might also enjoy making more and selling it to improve your bottom line. Not all soap recipes are created equal, however. Goat milk soap should lather well, rinse clean, and leave skin softer and moisturized. You can find plenty of recipes online and in other books, but later in this section, I give you my recipe for the best goat milk soap I've ever made.

Soap-making has a rather steep learning curve. Read through all of the instructions in this section before you start a recipe. And it's better to learn the techniques on cheap ingredients and very small batches. Buy small amounts of ingredients at first, and if you decide you want to go into high production later, consider getting oils in 5-gallon buckets to bring down costs.

If you're going to sell your soap for $4, $5, or $6 per bar, how you wrap it will make a big difference in the impression buyers get and how much they're willing to spend. Soap almost *must* be sold in person because it can only be appreciated if buyers can touch and smell it. Farmers' markets, craft shows, and a roadside stand might be places to sell your soap. Specialty gift shops will sometimes carry artisan soaps, too.

Goat milk soap is relatively easy to produce and makes a lovely bar when well packaged.

Essential Equipment

You don't need a lot of equipment to make soap, and you probably have most of it in your kitchen cabinets already. Following is a quick list of what you need.

- A heatproof stainless-steel, glass, or heat resistant (212°F) plastic container for mixing lye and milk; do not use aluminum, cast iron, or tin
- A large stainless-steel or enamel pot for melting the oils and mixing the soap
- Heavy-duty rubber spatulas or wooden spoons
- Stainless-steel wire whisk with a long handle
- Scale
- Soap mold
- Two candy thermometers that measure up to 220°F
- Safety goggles
- Rubber gloves

KIDDING AROUND

Soap molds can be anything from a Rubbermaid-type container to a wooden tray or even a heavy-duty cardboard box. Wood and cardboard need a plastic or wax-paper liner. Use your imagination, and be on the lookout for containers that will make nice molds. Opt for something flexible so the soap will come out easier with a little twist. Commercial molds are available, too, of course. For years, I used PVC downspout material cut into easy-to-handle lengths. Stand upright in a pan with ½ inch of melted wax. The cooled wax keeps the soap in the tube and then becomes the "pusher" you can use to remove the finished soap.

Safety First!

Before we go any further, we need to cover some safety information.

- Lye is caustic and burns skin. Keep it in a proper child- and airproof container. Be sure all members of your family know how dangerous it can be. Keep children and pets out of the work area until all the equipment is clean and put away.
- Keep pots/bowls away from the edge of the counter.
- Wear protective goggles, rubber gloves, and long sleeves.
- If you get lye on your skin, flush with vinegar and wash with soap and water.
- When mixing lye with milk, always add the lye to milk—not the other way around!

- Do not to inhale the dust when pouring the dry lye, and do not inhale the fumes off the milk-lye mixture. Work in a well-ventilated area, work with an exhaust hood nearby, or work outside to protect your lungs. The fumes dissipate shortly after the lye and milk are well mixed.

- Lay out all your equipment first, including getting your mold(s) ready.

- Measure the lye into a plastic container using a plastic scoop. Do not use these for other purposes.

- Be sure to tare, or zero-out, the scale first with the container when weighing lye, milk, or oils.

Mixing Things Up

Mixing lye and liquid creates lots of heat. When making soap with milk alone (no water), put the milk in the freezer and freeze to a slushy, near-frozen state. Then put the container in an ice water bath in the sink. Very slowly add the lye to the icy milk, stirring constantly, to keep the temperature from climbing. That might take 10 to 15 minutes. Do not breathe the fumes.

Be sure to keep the milk's temperature under 120°F. Cool it down to about 90°F to 95°F, at which point you can start heating up the oils to melt them. If the milk is kept cool enough, it will stay white or if warmed a bit, a lemon yellow. If the milk turns orange, dark orange, or brown, you should pour it down the drain and start again because you'll never get a quality product with scorched milk proteins.

Full milk is trickier to keep from scorching, but not if you add the lye very slowly.

When the oils have reached 85°F to 90°F, check the lye temperature. If it becomes too cool, place the container in another container filled with hot water. Do not heat the lye in a microwave or on the stove.

When the correct temperatures have been reached, add a fragrance oil to the oils, and pour the lye mixture very slowly into the oils, stirring constantly. At 85 degrees, this process may only take a few minutes. If either mixture is warmer, it may take a little longer to reach trace. Some fragrance oils will cause the soap to suddenly solidify.

Stir continuously with a stainless-steel whisk until the soap reaches *trace*, or when it reaches the point at which it leaves a mark when it's dripped over the surface of the soap in the container.

> **DEFINITION**
>
> **Trace** is the point at which the soap thickens just enough so if you drizzle soap onto the surface of the pot contents, it leaves a mark before disappearing. You pour soap into molds at trace.

Immediately pour soap into molds. Some recipes call for covering your molds to keep heat in. My recipe doesn't. Leave the soap undisturbed for at least 24 hours. Some fragrance oils produce a soap that needs two days to set up. The soap should be firm with no pools of oil on top.

Remove the soap from the molds and slice into bars if needed. If you have trouble getting the soap out of the mold, try placing the mold in the freezer overnight, and it should then pop out easily.

Place bars in an out-of-the-way place to cure for two or three weeks. You can check to see if it has cured by washing your hands with it. If it leaves a slimy feeling, leave it to cure for another week. My recipe needs far less curing than most recipes but still improves with curing.

Tips for Better Soap

All soaps heat up in the mold (exothermic reaction), but milk soaps generally heat up more. This is a good thing. Heated high enough, soaps go through a gel phase in the mold, and the *saponification* process goes faster. If you use plastic downspouts or Rubbermaid drawer dividers as molds, insulate lightly; otherwise, the high heat may distort the plastic molds.

Old-time soap makers used to use the "tongue test" on their soaps to test for mildness—and we newer ones still do! After unmolding your finished soap, touch a bar to your tongue. If it tingles, the soap contains excess lye and it either needs to saponify longer (keep checking as it cures) or you've got too much lye in the recipe and it will be caustic. In the latter case, grate it up when it's cured and use it for laundry detergent, mixed with a bit of borax.

Superfatting is the addition of more oil to the soap than there's lye to saponify it. The Majestic Mountain Sage calculator (www.thesage.com/calcs/lyecalc2.php) shows you different superfatting levels for a particular recipe.

DEFINITION

Saponification is the chemical reaction that happens between a lye solution and oils to make soap. **Superfatting** means putting more oil in the soap than the lye will saponify. Up to a point, a little superfatting makes the soap more luxurious and moisturizing.

Remember, when working with milk, that the butterfat is generally not accounted for in calculating the amount of lye to use. I've found that more superfatting is not better. Excess fats in milk soaps lead to problems with rancidity or a faint sour milk smell that can be noted on the skin when you sweat (not good!). Too much excess oil also reduces the soap's lathering ability.

Some fragrance oils speed up trace or cause the soap to seize and make it difficult to get the soap into the mold fast enough. Cassia or cinnamon/orange soaps can give you such trouble. I have found a simple trick to help avoid this: hold back 1 cup melted oils and premix the fragrance into this. Then at trace, add this last bit to the mix and stir well. This really makes a difference with tricky fragrances. It's a good practice with any new fragrance until you know how it works in your recipe. Most fragrance vendors will now tell you if a fragrance speeds up trace.

Making soap is an enjoyable creative venture and has the possibility for income potential. I recommend you read as much as you can find about making soap from the many soap-making books and websites available. If you can, watch someone with experience before you try on your own.

And now, without further ado, here's the best homemade goat milk soap recipe I've ever made:

Homemade Goat Milk Soap

This wonderfully moisturizing goat milk soap bar lathers well, rinses well, and leaves skin softer and feeling younger. Your skin will be so soft and moist, you can give up moisturizers forever! All ingredients are all by exact weight.

Yield:
18 to 24 (4-ounce) bars

28 ounces milk (or 3 ounces powdered goat milk and 25 ounces distilled water; mix powdered milk with oils and distilled water instead of liquid milk)

9.2 ounces lye

1 or 2 ounces fragrance, depending on how strong it is and how strong you like it

12 ounces coconut oil

28 ounces olive oil

12 ounces palm kernel oil

12 ounces palm oil

Prepare as directed in the previous sections. This is a low-temperature recipe, and all ingredients are mixed when they're about 85°F.

GOAT HORN

Working with lye, which is very caustic, can be very dangerous if not used correctly. Lye heats up dramatically when it comes into contact with liquid. Start with nearly frozen milk (in the slushy ice stage) in a heat-resistant plastic, ceramic, or stainless container. Do not use aluminum or cast-iron because lye reacts with both. Add lye very slowly to the frozen milk, and mix thoroughly as you go. Don't mix milk into lye—*it could explode!* The more slowly you add the lye to the slushy milk, the less chance it will raise the temperature of the milk high enough to scorch it.

More on Making Money with Your Goats

You might be wondering if there any other moneymaking possibilities with your goats. Yes! Many!

Some of the things already covered in Chapter 9 can be extended here to money-making possibilities. While none of these things are likely to make you rich, especially on a small scale, you may be able to add a little income from several of these ideas.

Selling Goat Milk and Cheese

If your state allows raw milk sales from the farm, and your milk is scrupulously clean and tasty, you may find customers for the extra milk you have. What do you charge for it? That depends, but it ought to be considerably more than what cow's milk in the store costs. I recently bought goat milk for $8 a gallon and was delighted to find it … and pay it.

If your state doesn't allow raw milk sales for human consumption, sometimes you can sell it labeled "for pet use only." Some states require the milk be colored, but usually you can use nontoxic coloring like carotene. And some people need goat milk for pets, for orphaned animals, or for special-needs animals.

Some goat owners sell a "share" of a goat to people who want goat milk. The goat remains at your place, but they can then get some of the milk from her because they're part owner of the goat. You'll have to figure out what to charge for the share, for the goat's upkeep, and for your work. For more information on raw milk and goat shares, check out the Weston A. Price Foundation website at www.realmilk.com/where2.html. You can also Google "goat shares" or read more about raw milk at www.rawmilk.org.

If you love making goat milk cheese but don't want to go to the trouble and expense of the Grade A requirements to be commercial, most states allow you to sell cheese that's been aged for 60 days. Be sure to research the regulations in your own state before embarking on a cheese-making venture, though. Goat milk cheeses are very popular, and you may be able to find a variety many people would love to buy from you. I have a friend whose homemade goat milk cheese sells for $16 a pound!

Feeding Other Animals

With your extra milk, you may be able to develop a following of people, rescue shelters, or veterinarians whose clients have an occasional orphan such as a foal whose mother has died or an alpaca baby in need of supplemental milk. A zoo or wild animal park may have a need for goat milk. Contact dog breeders, too. Let them all know you have goat milk available, and be sure to have it on hand—always—even if it's frozen.

Extra milk used to raise a calf or pigs can be expanded beyond just the meat your own family can eat. Pigs love the whey you get from making cheese, and it's good for them. The pork raised on whey or whole milk is absolutely delicious. You could raise more, and sell halves or quarters of those food animals when they're butchered. Both calves and piglets do very well on goat milk, and the resulting meat is very desirable and marketable. Chickens will also drink milk and whey—they'll even consume it if it's soured. Pigs will drink soured milk as well.

Goat Meat Possibilities

If you butcher goats beyond what you want for your family's use, like raising calves and pigs, you may find customers who want to buy some goat meat from you, or even a whole goat. There is some demand for whole carcasses for ethnic holidays and ritual celebrations. Many breeders will raise a few wethers to sell live to people wanting meat, for them to take and butcher themselves. In addition, you might experiment with making goat ham or jerky and find there is demand for either of those.

Please check your local and state regulations because it might not be legal in your area. In most places, you would need to have these products made in a plant that's inspected and licensed.

Best of the Breed: Breeding Stock

Goats who look good and perform their functions well (milk, meat, brush removal, or fiber), and particularly if they are winning ribbons in goat shows, have the potential to be breeding stock for sale to other farms or families. If you're enjoying the shows and doing well, you may have extra income from selling a few of the extra kids.

Making Money with Fertilizer

That composted pile of goat manure could potentially bring in some income. Whether you offer it by the you-shovel truckload or bag some and sell it at craft fairs or events, some people will pay for the organic fertilizer. Fertilizer may be regulated in your state, so check the requirements. This isn't a huge money-maker, but can bring in a little cash and provides some humor and good PR.

Maybe you've heard about raising worms with the manure. Even if you haven't, it's a simple process. Worm castings usually bring $1.50 per quart. Breeder worms bring about $25 per pound. Selling small amounts to fishermen is usually more lucrative, as the worms are in great demand if you're in an area near fishing spots.

Participating in Petting Zoos

For farms that have many species, a petting zoo of cute, friendly baby animals of several species might make a nice little petting zoo. I've seen petting zoos at many events, fenced where hundreds of children can interact with the animals. If you think your location might attract enough children to make it worth trying, give it a shot!

Few people have enough different species to consider this option, but perhaps you have neighbors with other species who will cooperate.

Just be certain you have adequate liability insurance in case of an incident. Baby goats have sharp teeth, and bunnies can bite or scratch!

Carting and Packing with Goats

If you've trained your goats to pull a cart, you might be able to capitalize on that goat and cart. Many people, especially children (well, their parents), would probably pay to go for a goat-cart ride or get their picture taken in the goat cart. Finding the right location for such an endeavor might be the biggest challenge. Explore public events such as fairs, craft shows, vintage events, farmers' markets, school events—anyplace where the public congregates and your goat cart could draw attention.

For people with pack goats who live near wilderness hiking areas, you could become an outfitter (guide) and manage trips into the wilderness with your string of pack goats. As mentioned earlier, goats are more "green," and that novelty might appeal to some hikers more than other types of packing.

Brush-Clearing with Goats

If you end up with a lot of goats and feel comfortable moving them to another piece of land for hire, this could be a potential money-maker for you. People who want brush, weeds, and scrub cleared off their land will sometimes prefer it be done by goats than by heavy equipment.

If you decide to freelance out your goats, you might also have to put up fences at the site (usually some kind of moveable electric fence) and you'll have to transport your goats there and back. You'll also have to find a way to keep them enclosed and safe. If you're not staying with the goats night and day, a livestock guardian dog might be necessary.

KIDDING AROUND

I once interviewed a gentleman who did this kind of work, and I learned that most of the charge for his service was actually for the prep work he had to do— fences, transport, etc. A few big companies have hundreds or even thousands of goats available for hire for brush-clearing. Someone with only a few goats probably couldn't make it pay because the clearing would be too slow. Nevertheless, it's an interesting and potentially profitable income option for those with, say, 40 to 100 goats.

Marketing, Marketing, Marketing

It's all well and good to talk about some of the income potential goats can provide. Having a good product (your goats and the products you get from them) is the first "leg" of any business. A second is the financials—the capital and record-keeping. Another leg, one that too often gets overlooked, is that the product does not sell itself; it needs your effective marketing. You have to learn how to convince someone that your product provides enough value for him so he's happy to trade his money for it.

Ready for a marketing secret that's sure to get results? Remember that marketing isn't about you; it's about the customer. People have a tendency to talk about themselves and their products, but your customer only cares about you or your stuff in terms of what it does to make *him* feel better or make *his* life better. This is called putting the emphasis on the benefits, not the features (the factual things). So if you have a goat for sale, you need to tell potential buyers she'll provide better economics for them because she gives such good milk in great quantities. Don't start with the fact that she gives a lot of milk but with the benefit of better economics (or nutrition or fun).

There's a great deal more information about marketing you may need if you decide to market your goat products. See Appendix B for books on marketing, or check out beyondthesidewalk.com.

The Intangibles of the Goat Lifestyle

Whether you take care of your goats before you go to a "regular" kind of job and after you get home at night or you're home with them all day, they provide tremendous lifestyle benefits.

Physical contact with goats is a huge stress-reducer. Petting them, scratching their ears, and the sensory experience of the milking routine all reduce the stresses of the day. Some people claim it's better than therapy!

And goat antics are enormously entertaining. The outdoor nature of the work of goats is both good for you and enjoyable in its own right. If your goats are tame and bonded to you, you'll share definite companionship when you deal with them on their terms.

Goats appeal to people who have a strong sense of independence and who enjoy a lifestyle where they feel they have control of some basics. The lifestyle that goes along with goats includes the satisfaction of controlling where some of your food and household products come from and knowing what's in those foods. It also promotes skills and values of an older, slower, nostalgic time.

The intangibles of the goat lifestyle might not appeal to everyone, but for those who appreciate it, these things are invaluable. The people living this way wouldn't trade a minute for a different kind of life.

Raising goats fits well with family life.
(Colette Kemper)

The bottom line is that goats can help improve your bottom line in monetary ways as well as in ways that feed your family and even feed your soul! May you have great fun, productivity, and maybe even some help with your finances from your goats!

The Least You Need to Know

- Goat shows are fun, a good place to learn more about goats, and fodder for folks with a strong competitive interest.
- Goat meat is delicious and healthy for those who are willing to butcher.

- If you're up for some hard but satisfying work, you can try your hand at making goat leather.
- Your goats will provide plenty of wonderful organic fertilizer for your gardening needs.
- Goat cart-pulling has a long history and provides a lot of fun, and packing into the wilderness with goats is a "greener" alternative to horse packing.
- Goats are well suited to 4-H and FFA livestock projects.
- Many goat-related products, activities, and projects can contribute to your income stream.
- Living with goats offers many soul-satisfying perks.

Glossary

anthelmintics or **antihelminthics**   Drugs that expel parasitic worms (helminths) from the body, by either stunning or killing them.

attachments   The ligaments that hold the udder to the goat's body either tightly or loosely.

banding   A method of neutering a young buck by cutting off blood flow to the testicles so they wither and drop off.

booster   A second, third, or annual vaccination shot that "boosts" the effectiveness of the vaccine in preventing a disease.

breeding season   The period of seasonal fertility, usually from August to January, when goats breed and conceive.

browse   A category of plants that includes brush (woody plants) and forbs (broadleafed, nongrassy plants). It's the preferred food for goats.

buck   A male goat.

burdizo   A tool for castrating that crushes the blood supply and spermatic cords so the testicles wither and fall off.

cabrito   Meat from a goat kid between 4 and 8 weeks old.

California mastitis test (CMT)   A first-line do-at-home test for milk quality.

Caprinae   The scientific name of the subfamily into which goats are classified; the genus is *Capra*.

caprine   A word to identify things relating to goats.

caprine arthritis encephalitis (CAE)   A viral disease in goats that can cause debilitating arthritis, pneumonia, low milk production, and encephalitis. It's passed in colostrum, milk, and bodily fluids.

capriole   A vertical jump with a kick of the hind legs at the top of the jump, a typical baby goat maneuver.

carotenes   The precursors of vitamin A. These colorful compounds give carrots their orange color and are found in many colorful fruits and vegetables. Carotenes are converted to vitamin A (colorless) in goat milk products, making them white where cow products would be yellow or yellowish.

carotenoids   The entire group of carotenes.

caseous lymphadenitis (CL)   A disease in goats that causes quarter- to lime-size abscesses in the lymph nodes. It's extremely contagious.

chevon   Meat from a goat older than 8 weeks of age.

chèvre   The French word for "goat." Refers to cheese made from goat milk.

Clostridium   A class of bacteria that causes enterotoxemia, tetanus, gas gangrene, and botulism.

COB   The designation for any grain mixture of corn, oats, and barley.

coccidia   One-celled parasitic organisms that do damage to the digestive tract of goats. They can be treated with sulfa compounds.

colostrum   The thick yellowish first milk produced by mammals. It's full of antibodies that protect newborns.

dairy clip   A partial haircut for a milking goat that removes the long hair around her udder and back end to keep milk cleaner.

dairy ration   A grain combination that includes an additional protein supplement to raise the protein level of the grain.

dam   A goat's mother.

dehorning   The process of surgically removing horns from a grown animal.

dewclaw   The bump on the back side of the foot where the pastern connects.

disbudding   The process of cauterizing the blood supply to a horn before it starts growing. It's done with a disbudding iron that gets nearly red hot.

doe   A female goat.

dystochia   The medical term for a difficult labor and birth. Usually occurs when multiple fetuses are tangled or positioned poorly.

estrus   Heat cycles and the physiologic changes that occur to enable a pregnancy.

fitting   The process of preparing a goat for show. It includes hair clipping, general cleaning, and hoof trimming.

goat berry   A goat's fecal matter, or manure.

heat cycles   The 18 to 21 days between "heats," which are the 2 or 3 days when a doe is receptive to the buck.

heritability   The degree to which a trait depends on genetics rather than environment and management.

hock   The joint in a goat's back leg, similar to your elbow.

hoof wall   The tough outer layer of the goat hoof, similar in texture and composition to your fingernails.

horn bud   The developing horn of a newborn goat. It feels like a slight bump or button under the skin.

hypocalcemia   The condition of not having enough calcium. Calcium is critical in muscle function, so a goat short on calcium will get shaky and then be unable to get up. If the situation isn't corrected, eventually the heart (a muscle) will stop.

ketosis   A metabolic condition that occurs when a goat stops eating and her body begins metabolizing its own fat reserves. It's always secondary to other health issues and is frequently fatal.

kid   A baby goat.

kidded; kidding   The birth process in goats.

lactation   The term for the time a mammal is producing milk. In goats, it starts when her kids are born. Dairy goats tend to give milk for a 10-month period (usually 305 days) before they rest for 60 days, produce kids again, and start over. Meat goats tend to produce milk until their kids are weaned, usually 3 or 4 months.

legume hay   Any hay made from a plant that produces a seed pod such as alfalfa, peas, peanuts, or clover.

livestock guardian dogs (LGD)   Dogs bred to be both predator deterrents and protectors for sheep and goats.

mastitis   The name for any infection in the udder.

medial suspensory ligament   The connective tissue that holds the goat's udder to her body. It connects in the front of her udder and in the back through the center of her udder.

medium-chain fatty acids   The good fatty acids. They are more easily burned as fuel in human nutrition than stored as fat.

one-day tests   A period of 24 hours during which a goat's milk is weighed, tested for butterfat and protein, and recorded for official production records.

open classes   A show where the quality of the goat is judged, not the accuracy of the handler. This is not restricted by the age of the person exhibiting; it's not necessarily a youth or 4-H show.

orifice   The hole in the end of the teat through which milk comes out.

pannier   A bag or basket that attaches to a goat's pack saddle for carrying your stuff on the goat's back.

parasites   Animals that live in your goat's tissues or steal her nutritional intake. They cause lost production, disease, and death.

pastern   The short bone that connects the goat's leg bones to the hoof. It's angled slightly to provide shock absorption.

pinkeye   A bacterial infection of the goat's eyes that causes them to water and turn red. It can eventually cause blindness if left untreated.

precocious udder   A condition of premature udder development in a young doe who has not been bred. It may run in families. Unless her udder has heat or sensitivity (mastitis), it should be left alone and will eventually continue to mature after she is bred.

reasons   The comments made by the judge at a goat show that explains why he placed goats in a particular order in the lineup.

replacer   A powdered preparation mixed with water meant to replace milk to feed kids. If you must use replacer, only use those made from milk, not soy or grains.

ruminants   Animals who have four stomachs and chew their cud.

rut   The season of a buck's interest in the opposite sex. It corresponds to the breeding season.

sanctioned show   A goat show that's been approved by the sponsoring organization and makes the results official.

saponification The chemical reaction that happens between a lye solution and oils to make soap.

scurs Distorted horn growths after incomplete disbudding. They grow in weird shapes and directions, sometimes into a part of the skull or neck of the goat and could kill if not removed.

setup The way a goat is positioned in the show ring when she is standing in place. Her head should be up, her feet squarely placed, and her topline nice and straight.

silent heat When a doe shows no signs of heat even though she is physiologically "in heat."

sire A goat's father.

smallholder A holding of agricultural land smaller than a small farm.

strip cup A cup covered by a screen, which is used for the first couple squirts of milk at milking time to check for clots or abnormal milk.

structural soundness The components of a goat's skeleton that make her body work smoothly and healthily and give her longevity without aches and pains.

superfatting Putting more oil in soap than the lye will saponify. Up to a point, a little superfatting makes the soap more luxurious and moisturizing.

teat dip An antibacterial liquid used to cover the teat ends after milking to protect against bacterial invasion into the udder.

teats The "handles" on the goat's udder for milking or the elongated nipples the kids nurse from.

tetanus A clostridial bacteria disease that's nearly always fatal. It causes stiffness, light and sound sensitivity, and eventually death.

third-cutting hay The hay produced when alfalfa is cut for the third time. The stems are fine enough that your goats will eat all of it, stems and all. Third-cutting also has a higher protein content than earlier cuttings.

topline Another name for the entire backbone, from withers to hips.

trace The point at which soap thickens just enough so that if you drizzle soap onto the surface of the pot contents, it leaves a mark before disappearing. At trace, you can pour your soap into the mold.

udder The mammary gland and storage organ for milk.

vaccinations   Shots designed to create immunity to diseases common among goats.

weigh tape   A tape measure used around the rib cage just behind the front legs to estimate the goat's weight. The measurement corresponds to an approximate weight.

wether   A neutered male goat.

withers   The top of a goat's shoulder assembly. It's a bump at the beginning of the topline and where the neck and shoulders connect. Withers should be the high point of the back.

Resources

The following resources can help you find additional information and tools or products you may need. These are not the only resources for goat aficionados, but they are some of the best.

Registry Organizations

American Boer Association
232 W. Beauregard, Suite 104
San Antonio, TX 76903
915-486-2242
info@abga.org
www.abga.org

American Dairy Goat Association
PO Box 865
Spindale, NC 28160
www.adga.org

American Goat Society
PO Box 330
Broad Run, VA 20137
www.americangoatsociety.com

American Kiko Goat Association (AKGA)
PO Box 531
Gordonsville, VA 22942
541-967-5380
www.kikogoats.com

Colored Angora Goat Breeders Association
www.cagba.org

International Kiko Goat Association (IKGA)
PO Box 677
Jonesborough, TN 37659
1-888-538-4279
www.theikga.org

Kinder Goat Breeders Association
PO Box 1575
Snohomish, WA 98291
kindergoatbreeders.com

Miniature Dairy Goats
PO Box 7244
Kennewick, WA 99336-0616
509-591-4256
www.miniaturedairygoats.com

National Pygmy Goat Association
1932 149th Avenue SE
Snohomish, WA 98290
www.npga-pygmy.com

PCA Goats
info@pcagoats.org or registrar@
pcagoats.org

Pygora Breeders Association
538 Lamson Road
Lysander, NY 13027
315-678-2812
pbaregistrar@aol.com
www.pygoragoats.org

United States Boer Goat Association
PO Box 100
Spicewood, TX 78669
866-66-USBGA (866-668-7242)
www.usbga.org

Livestock Supplies

Caprine Supply
PO Box Y
DeSoto, KS 66018
1-800-646-7735
www.caprinesupply.com

Hamby Dairy Supply
2402 S.W. Water Street
Maysville, MO 64469
1-800-306-8937
www.hambydairysource.com

Hoegger Goat Supply
1-800-221-4628
www.hoeggergoatsupply.com

Jeffers Supply
PO Box 100
Dothan, AL 36302
1-800-533-3377
www.jefferslivestock.com

Mary Kellogg's Goat Minerals
RR1-Box 66
Manchester, OK 73758
580-694-2372
thekelloggcenter@hotmail.com or
acfdirector2000@yahoo.com

Nasco Supply
1-800-558-9595
www.enasco.com/prod/Home

Omaha Vaccine
11143 Mockingbird Drive
Omaha, NE 68137-2332
1-800-367-4444
www.omahavaccine.com

PBS Animal Health
2780 Richville Drive SE
Massillon, OH 44646
1-800-321-0235
www.pbsanimalhealth.com

Premier1Supplies
2031 300th Street
Washington, Iowa 52353
1-800-282-6631
www.premier1supplies.com

Registers Sheep and Goat Supplies
3398 Gabe Smith Road
Wade, NC 28395
1-888-310-9606
goatsupplies.netfirms.com

Sydell, Inc.
46935 SD Highway 50
Burbank, SD 57010
1-800-842-1369
www.sydell.com

Cheese-Making Supplies

Cheesemaking Supply Outlet
9155 Madison Road
Montville, OH 44064
440-968-3770
rmhcso@alltel.net

Glengarry Cheesemaking and Dairy Supplies
RR#2
Alexandria, Ontario
Canada
K0C 1A0
613-525-3133
fax: 613-525-3394
morris@cnwl.igs.net
www.glengarrycheesemaking.on.ca

Leeners
9293 Olde Eight Road
Northfield, OH 44067
1-800-543-3697
www.leeners.com/cheese.html

New England Cheesemaking Supply Co.
PO Box 85
Ashfield, MA 01330
413-628-3808
www.cheesemaking.com

Soap-Making Supplies and Recipes

About.com's Candle and Soap Making
candleandsoap.about.com/od/
soapmakingbasics/u/soapuserpath1.htm

Bramble Berry, Inc.
2139 Humbolt Street
Bellingham, WA 98225
360-734-8278
www.brambleberry.com

Majestic Mountain Sage
918 West 700 North, Suite 104
Logan, UT 84321
435-755-0863
www.thesage.com

Miller's Homemade Soap Pages
www.millersoap.com/#Soap

Rainbow Meadow, Inc.
4494 Brooklyn Road
Jackson, MI 49201
1-800-207-4047
www.rainbowmeadows.com

Snowdrift Farm, Inc.
2750 South 4th Avenue, Suites 107
and 108
Tucson, AZ 85713
1-888-999-6950
www.snowdriftfarm.com

Southern Garden Scents
PO Box 175
Eastman, GA 31023
478-448-1346
orders@southerngardenscents.com
southerngardenscents.com

Sweet Cakes Soapmaking Supplies
952-945-9900
www.sweetcakes.com

Teach Soap
www.teachsoap.com

Magazines

Dairy Goat Journal
145 Industrial Drive
Medford, WI 54451
www.dairygoatjournal.com
$21/year

The Goat Magazine
PO Box 2694
San Angelo, TX 76902
325-653-5438
www.goatmagazine.info
$24/year

Goat Rancher
225 Hankins Road
Sarah, MS 38665
www.goatrancher.com
$29/year

Ruminations
PO Box 859
Ashburnham, MA 01430
Editor@smallfarmgoat.com
978-827-1305
www.smallfarmgoat.com
$25/year

United Caprine News
PO Box 328
Crowley, TX 76036
www.unitedcaprinenews.com
$22.50/year

Wild Fibers Magazine
PO Box 1752
Rockland, ME 04841
207-785-3932
www.wildfibersmagazine.com
$28/year

Book Suppliers

Caprine Supply
www.caprinesupply.com

Dairy Goat Journal Books
www.dairygoatjournal.com/bookstore.
html

Hamby Dairy Supply
www.hambydairysource.com

Hoegger Supply Co.
www.hoeggergoatsupply.com

Supplies for Packing and Carts

Equestrian International
116 King Court
New Holland, PA 17557
717-355-2900
1-800-632-4805
www.horsetackinternational.com/
Amish-goat-carts-and-pumpkin-wagon-
large-rustic-finish.html?currency=USD

H S Horse Cart
www.hscart.com/dog-cart.html

Hoegger Goat Supply
1-800-221-4628
www.hoeggergoatsupply.com/xcart/
home.php?cat=24

Nikki's Pony Express
www.nikkisponyexpress.com/
oakminicarts.html

Northwest Packgoats
Weippe, ID
1-888-PACKGOAT (1-888-722-5462)
www.northwestpackgoats.com

Owyhee Packgoat Supply
15985 S. Indiana Avenue
Caldwell, ID 83607
208-454-2015
gdlocati@cableone.net
www.owyheepackgoatsupplies.com

Wind River Pack Goats
280 North 9th Street
Lander, WY 82520
307-332-3328
www.goatpacking.com

Working Goats
www.workinggoats.com/?id=80

For Further Reading

Belanger, Jerry. *Storey's Guide to Raising Milk Goats.* North Adams, MA: Storey
    Publishing, 2000.

Blowey, Roger, and Peter Edmondson. *Mastitis Control in Dairy Herds.* Ipswich,
    England: Farming Press Limited, 2000.

Bowman, Gail. *Raising Meat Goats for Profit.* Meridian, ID: Bowman Communication
    Press, 2000.

Carroll, Ricki. *Home Cheese Making*. North Adams, MA: Storey Publishing, 2002.

Considine, Harvey. *Dairy Goats for Pleasure and Profit*. Lake Mills, WI: Dairy Goat Journal Publishing Corporation, 2005.

Considine, Harvey, and George Trimberger. *Dairy Goat Judging Techniques*. Scottsdale, AZ: Dairy Goat Journal Publishing Corporation, 1985.

Fink, Linda. *Life in the Goat Lane*. Grand Ronde, OR: Linda Fink, 1990.

Foreyt, William J. *Veterinary Parasitology Reference Manual*. Hoboken, NJ: Blackwell Professional Publishing, John Wiley & Sons, Inc., 2002.

Guss, Samuel. *Management and Diseases of Dairy Goats*. Scottsdale, AZ: Dairy Goat Journal Pub. Corp., 1977.

Haenlein, George. *Extension Goat Handbook*. Washington, DC: Department of Agriculture, 1983.

Heatherington, Lois. *All About Goats*. Ipswich, England: Farming Press Limited, 1992.

Jackson, Robert, and Alice Hall. *Fundamentals of Improved Dairy Goat Management*. San Bernardino, CA: Hall Press, 1986.

Lutman, Gail. *Raising Milk Goats Successfully*. Carmel, NY: Ideals Publishing, 1986.

Makela, Casey. *Milk-Based Soaps: Making Natural, Skin-Nourishing Soap*. North Adams, MA: Storey Publishing, 1997.

Merck Veterinary Manual, 50th Edition. Duluth, GA: Merck & Co., Inc., 2008.

Mionczynski, John. *Pack Goat*. Boulder, CO: Pruett Publishing Company, 1992.

Mitcham, Stephanie, and Allison Mitcham. *The Angora Goat: Its History, Management and Diseases*. Sumner, IA: Crane Creek Publications, 1999.

Owen, Nancy Lee. *Illustrated Standard of the Dairy Goat*. Scottsdale, AZ: Dairy Goat Journal Publishing Corporation, 1986.

Philpot, W. Nelson, and S. C. Nickerson. *Winning the Fight Against Mastitis*. Holmen, WI: Westphalia Surge, 2000.

Pugh, D. G. *Sheep and Goat Medicine*. Philadelphia, PA: Elsevier Health Sciences, 2001.

Sayer, Maggie. *Storey's Guide to Raising Meat Goats: Managing, Breeding, Marketing*. North Adams, MA: Storey Publishing, 2007.

Sinn, Rosalie. *Raising Goats for Milk and Meat*. Little Rock, AR: Heifer International, 1983.

Smith, Mary, and David Sherman. *Goat Medicine*. Baltimore, MD: Lippincott Williams and Wilkins, 1994.

Spaulding, C. E., DVM. *A Veterinary Guide for Animal Owners*. Emmaus, PA: Rodale Press, 1976.

Thedford, Thomas. *Goat Health Handbook*. Morrilton, AR: Winrock International, 1983.

Trew, Sally W., with Zonella B. Gould. *The Complete Idiot's Guide to Making Natural Soaps*. Indianapolis: Alpha Books, 2010.

Weaver, Sue. *Get Your Goat!* North Adams, MA: Storey Publishing, 2010.

———. *Storey's Guide to Raising Miniature Livestock*. North Adams, MA: Storey Publishing, 2009.

Winslow, Ellie. *Making Money with Goats, Sixth Edition*. Reno, NV: Beyond the Sidewalk Publishing, 2007.

Index

Get back to the simpler things in life.

Reap a bountiful harvest from your own backyard!

Vegetable Gardening

Daria Price Bowman and Carl A. Price

978-1-59257-907-5

Fulfill your dream of open space and quiet days

Country Living

Fulfill your dream of open space and quiet days

Live a simpler, less dependent lifestyle—without feeling deprived

Self-Sufficient Living

Jerome D. Belanger

978-1-59257-945-7

Can it. Freeze it. Pickle it. Preserve it. Here's how.

Preserving Food

Enjoy the fruits of your labor all year long

Year-Round Gardening

Delilah Smittle and Sheri Ann Richerson

978-1-59257-970-9

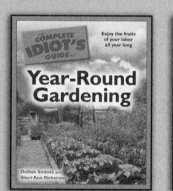

Jerome D. Belanger

978-1-59257-986-0

James R. Leverentz

978-1-61564-009-6

Everything the budding beekeeper needs for a healthy, productive hive

Beekeeping

Dean Stiglitz and Laurie Herboldsheimer

978-1-61564-011-9

"Everything you need to know to get started and keep composting successfully."
—Jon Lamp? (aka "Jen gardener"), author of The Green Gardener's Guide

Composting

Turn your organic waste material into black gold

Chris McLaughlin

978-1-61564-008-9

Live greener—and cleaner—with your own handcrafted soaps

Making Natural Soaps

Sally W. Trew with Zonella B. Gould

978-1-61564-022-5

Ditch the processed foods and get your fill of nutritious, all-natural foods

Eating Clean

Diane A. Welland, M.S., R.D.

978-1-59257-946-4

ALPHA

idiotsguides.com